People
to Know

People to Know

A supplement to
Childcraft–The How and Why Library

World Book, Inc.
a Scott Fetzer company
Chicago   London   Sydney   Toronto

Copyright © 1989
World Book, Inc.
Merchandise Mart Plaza, Chicago, Illinois 60654
All rights reserved
Printed in the United States of America
ISBN 0-7166-0689-5
Library of Congress Catalog Card No. 65-25105

# Contents

The publisher wishes to thank the following individuals for their gracious assistance in reviewing stories and helping with information: Beverly Cleary and David Reuther, Vice President and Editor in Chief, Morrow Junior Books; Carolyn Conrad and Janet Adams, I.M. Pei & Partners; Betty Fox; Judy Johnson, Executive Director of the Jane Goodall Institute for Wildlife Research, Education and Conservation; Justice Sandra Day O'Connor; Don N. Page, Professor of Physics, Pennsylvania State University, and Catherine Hotke-Page, M.D., associates and friends of Stephen Hawking; Rosa Parks; Sally K. Ride.

 # Preface

This is a book about people. The people are men and women who have helped us know more about the world, or who have proven they are so good at their work. Perhaps they are very brave people who have made life better for others, sometimes at great risk.

The stories take place over many years. People of today and of recent times begin the book, and the stories move back into time. Some of the stories are about the person's childhood; some are about what makes the person famous; others are just interesting stories about the person. Each selection is based carefully on fact, although many are written in a fictionalized style.

So, turn the pages and discover new people or learn something new about a person you already know. Who are your favorite "people to know," and what makes them special for you? Who else would you add that we could not include for reasons of space? Enjoy the book!

Stephen Hawking studies how the universe works.

Fortunate in Almost Every Respect

One October morning in 1987, Stephen Hawking sat before his computer. He was in his home in Cambridge, England. Nearby was his office at Cambridge University, where Stephen was a professor.

Stephen was almost finished writing a book. Unlike his other writings, this book was not for scientists. It was for all the nonscientists who wanted to know what he and other scientists were doing. In plain words and even

with a few jokes, Stephen had explained the basic forces of nature. For example, he discussed how gravity holds the planets in orbit around the sun. Stephen told, too, of his efforts to join what we know about nature into one explanation about the whole universe and how it began.

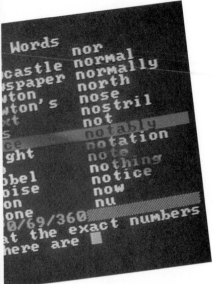

There are many ways to communicate. Stephen Hawking chooses words that appear in alphabetical lists on his computer screen. Then he puts them together in sentences, as a student watches.

This morning, Stephen hoped, he would complete his book. All that was left was the opening. He wanted to explain why he had written the book and to thank the people who had helped him.

For Stephen, writing this book was an unusual process. Because of a serious disease, he can't move his body the way most people can. He can't write with a pen or type keys on a computer. Instead, he worked a switch that controlled his computer. When he squeezed the switch, four columns of words appeared on the screen. More squeezes moved the cursor, a sort of flashing pointer, across the words until it stopped on the word he wanted and copied the word at the bottom of the screen. With his switch, Stephen changed the screen of columns to another group of words. Again he moved the cursor through the words to his choice and copied it at the bottom of the page. There. Another passage was done:

> Where did the universe come from? How and why did it begin? Will it come to an end, and if so, how? These are questions that are of interest to us all.

The medical name for Stephen's disease is amyotrophic lateral sclerosis (uh MY uh TRAHF ihk LAT uhr uhl sklih ROH sihs), or ALS. In England, it is called motor neuron disease. In America, it is also called Lou Gehrig's disease, after a famous baseball player who died of it. ALS gradually destroys the nerves and muscles needed for moving your body.

When Stephen graduated from college in 1962, he began work on a higher degree in physics. Physics has to do with how everything in nature works. Physicists study light, heat, sound, gravity, energy—and all kinds of questions about how the universe is made.

During his first year of study, he learned he had ALS. His doctors told him that he would see, hear, and taste as before. But soon he would not be able to walk, write, or even feed himself. He would probably die before he earned his degree.

For a while Stephen thought of giving up. For months he did almost nothing. Why bother working, if he would die so soon? But then he fell in love with Jane Wilde, a student studying languages in London. They decided to get married. Then Stephen wanted to finish his degree, work at Cambridge, and keep on living.

Two other things happened about this time, too. The disease slowed. It was clear that Stephen would live longer than was first thought. Also, Stephen became deeply interested in a strange idea that another scientist, Roger Penrose, had written about.

Penrose discussed black holes. These are unusual places that may exist in space. One way a black hole may form is when a huge star burns itself out and collapses. Black holes are areas in which gravity is terribly strong. Anything pulled into the black hole cannot get out again. Even time stops!

Stephen went back to his studies with new interest. First, he completed his thesis. That is the long paper that students must write to finish their advanced studies.

Then he began working at Cambridge and developing many more ideas about black holes and the nature of the universe. Eventually, ALS forced Stephen to get around in a motorized wheelchair. But this did not stop him from using his mind and presenting his ideas at scientific meetings

Of course, you can't really see a black hole! Scientists believe black holes are invisible places in space where gravity is so strong that not even light can escape.

Hawking's son Timmy stops in to see his father, and brings a pet rabbit along.

around the world. It was after a meeting in America that he decided to write his book for nonscientists.

When he started the book, Stephen was unable to write by hand at all. ALS had made his hands and arms too weak to hold a pen or to type. So he dictated the book to assistants. Then, while visiting Switzerland, he became ill with pneumonia. He had trouble breathing. An operation on his neck helped him recover from the pneumonia, but it left him without his voice.

Again Stephen was almost ready to give up. How could he finish his book—or do anything else—if he couldn't speak *or* write?

Now his friends in England and America joined to help him. They developed a special computer system and mounted it on his wheelchair. He was still strong enough to squeeze a switch. That was all he needed to operate his computer. He could put together words from his word list, or spell out words letter by letter. The words would appear on his computer screen. In addition, if he wanted to speak aloud, a voice synthesizer spoke the words for him!

The words Stephen was choosing this morning would be printed out and sent to the publisher of his book. He finished the opening. Now he went back over it to make sure it was right. He changed a few words. In another paragraph he put in a comma. There. The corrected sentence was just what he wanted to say:

> Apart from being unlucky enough to get ALS, or motor neuron disease, I have been fortunate in almost every other respect.

Stephen Hawking
(1942-   )

Dr. Stephen Hawking is considered one of the world's most brilliant living scientists. Despite being handicapped by ALS, he has had a successful career as a university professor and physicist. He also has enjoyed a happy family life with his wife, Jane, and three children, Robert, Lucy, and Timmy.

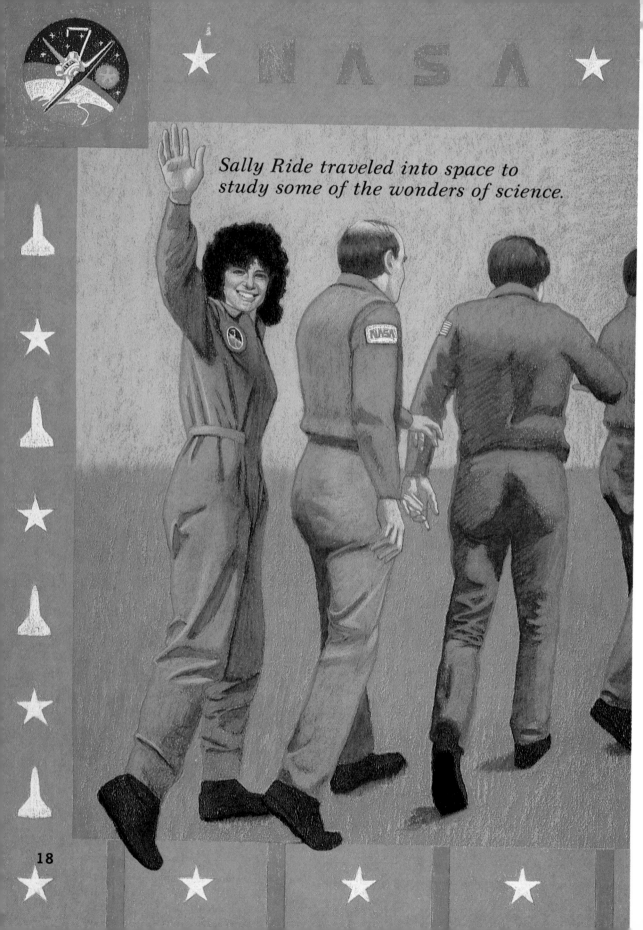

Sally Ride traveled into space to study some of the wonders of science.

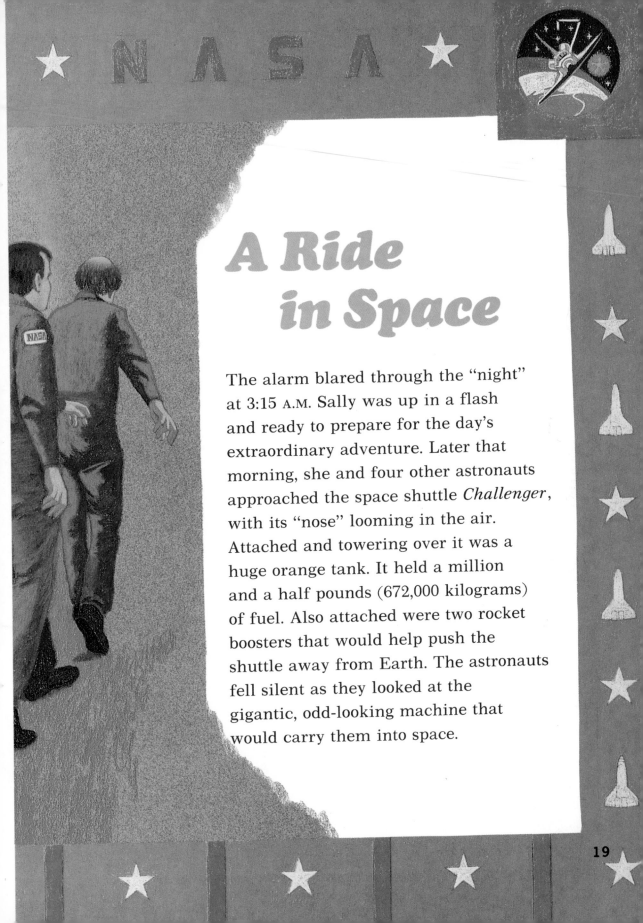

A Ride in Space

The alarm blared through the "night" at 3:15 A.M. Sally was up in a flash and ready to prepare for the day's extraordinary adventure. Later that morning, she and four other astronauts approached the space shuttle *Challenger*, with its "nose" looming in the air. Attached and towering over it was a huge orange tank. It held a million and a half pounds (672,000 kilograms) of fuel. Also attached were two rocket boosters that would help push the shuttle away from Earth. The astronauts fell silent as they looked at the gigantic, odd-looking machine that would carry them into space.

Sally had spent years training to be an astronaut and one whole year training just for this flight. Now, finally, the day was here. The astronauts stepped into an elevator and glided up the launch tower. Up at the nose of the space shuttle, assistants strapped the crew into their seats. They had to lie flat on their backs since the shuttle already was pointing up.

Ground control was busy making sure everything was okay. No problems were found. The crew was told "go for launch."

The countdown began. The shuttle's main engines fired. It made the whole shuttle shake and rattle. BLAST OFF!!

White smoke filled the air. The shuttle started to lift up off the ground.

There was a thundering noise inside the shuttle. Sally, seated directly behind the pilot and commander, felt the shaking and roaring and knew they were on their way.

You can see one of the two rocket boosters and the orange fuel tank here next to the space shuttle.

Two minutes after liftoff, the two rocket boosters fell away from the shuttle. The ride became smooth and quiet. But then, a few minutes later, the tremendous force of the launch started pushing against the astronauts' bodies. Sally felt very uncomfortable. She had to strain against the force to see the instrument panel.

Next, the big fuel tank fell away from the shuttle. The force of the launch ended and the astronauts became more comfortable.

Ground control was relieved. They radioed the crew. "How does it feel to fly into space?" they asked.

"Ever been to Disneyland?" Sally responded. "Well, this is definitely one of the best rides!"

Soon the shuttle was in orbit and the crew could leave their seats. Being in orbit meant that the shuttle was circling the Earth, traveling along a steady path. It was the Earth's gravity that kept the shuttle in orbit. Now came something Sally had been looking forward to all through training: weightlessness! In space, everything floats, even people. Sally tried "swimming" in the air. But she found that she had to push against a wall in order to get anywhere. She was soon used to it and started to have fun with it.

Now that Sally was adjusted to weightlessness, she turned to her other job on the shuttle. She was a mission specialist: a very smart, highly trained scientist. Over the next six days, the crew had to launch three satellites and recover one of them. Satellites are machines that "work" in space. They may take pictures and measurements that help us understand space and forecast weather. Other satellites send television and telephone signals all over the world.

Sally had worked hard before this flight on a giant robot arm called a remote manipulator (ma NIH pyoo lay tur) arm. The arm is controlled from the shuttle by an

During flight, Sally Ride communicates with ground control (above, left). Astronauts Hauck and Ride practice operating the robot arm during training (below, left). The arm (drawn above) is like a giant flexible crane that extends from the shuttle into space.

astronaut. It allows the astronaut to grab objects, such as satellites, from space and bring them to the shuttle.

On the fifth day of the mission, the astronauts released the last of the three satellites. It traveled in space next to the shuttle for a while. Then Sally used the robot arm to grab the satellite and bring it back to the shuttle. This was the first time anyone had used the arm to pick up an object in space.

This whole process was very important to the space program. It showed that broken satellites could be picked up and repaired in the space shuttle cargo area. This was a major accomplishment for the shuttle crew.

23

Weightlessness can mean being "upside down" when you eat!

At mealtimes, the astronauts took turns preparing food. Some of the food was dehydrated and stored in pouches. This means that all the water was removed from the food. The astronauts had to use a water gun to shoot water into the pouches before they could heat their meals. All the food had to be easy to hold on to, otherwise it would float away while the astronauts tried to eat! They could only drink by using straws, and they had to strap their special food trays onto their laps.

When it was time for bed, Sally gathered her sleeping bag and a tape player. Her sleeping bag would float. "It will be like sleeping on air," she thought. Sally liked to sleep right next to a window. Before falling asleep she would listen to music and watch Earth pass by beneath her.

For six days the astronauts circled the earth. They launched each satellite successfully. Then, at the end of the mission, the space team got ready to bring the shuttle back to Earth. The crew had to reenter the Earth's atmosphere. When they finally glided back down to the ground, it was in many ways like the way a jet airplane would land on a runway. Had Sally Ride enjoyed her time in space? She was ready to get in line for the next space flight!

Sally Ride
(1951-   )

On June 18, 1983, Sally Kristen Ride became the first American woman to travel in space. The other astronauts on the mission were commander Robert Crippen, co-pilot Frederick Hauck, and mission specialists John Fabian and Norman Thagard.

Shuttle commander Crippen, who chose Sally for this flight, said, "She is flying with us because she is the very best person for the job." Sally also was chosen because she is an expert in the use of the remote manipulator arm.

After the *Challenger* exploded in 1986, killing everyone on board, Sally Ride was appointed to a special group that tried to find the cause of the explosion. She also led a group that investigated America's future in space exploration after the *Challenger* explosion. Dr. Ride now is working at Stanford University's Center for International Security and Arms Control.

Walter Payton proved from the beginning of his career that he would be a great football player.

Rushing for the Record

"And starting at running back for the Chicago Bears . . . Number 34 . . . Walter Payton!"

As "Number 34" sprinted out onto the field that chilly afternoon—November 20, 1977—few people knew that Walter Payton had been ill with the flu just days before. He had missed parts of two practices.

Now it was Sunday. The Bears were facing the first-place Minnesota Vikings. They had just a two-game lead on the Bears. With a victory today, the Bears might have a chance to win the Central Division championship.

"I don't think I can do too much," Walter thought to himself. "I still feel under the weather." But then he remembered what his father had always said:

"Never settle for second best. Either do your best or don't try at all. And if you start something, make sure you finish it!"

Those words were still in Walter's mind as the Bears' quarterback called the first play. It was a run to the right side with Walter carrying the ball.

Walter felt the hard football being slammed into his stomach. Darting to his right, the young running back spotted an opening in the Vikings' tough defense. Walter's legs went into a full gallop, and he wasn't stopped until he had moved the ball 29 yards down the field.

"I think I'm feeling better," he thought as he jumped up from the ground. Walter Payton never spent much time on the ground after being tackled. Bouncing back up was one of his trademarks.

"Way to go," one of his teammates said to him. But Walter didn't reply. He almost never said a word while he was in action on the field. He was too busy concentrating on the game.

By the end of the first quarter, Payton had carried the ball 13 times for 77 yards. Many running backs don't get that many

yards in a whole game! Walter hardly
remembered feeling sick earlier.

By halftime, Payton had run for 144
yards. This was the Bears' 10th game of the
season, and it was the seventh time Walter
had carried the ball for more than 100
yards. During halftime, the Minnesota
Vikings discussed how to stop Number 34.

"We can play better than we did in the
first half," said a defensive lineman. "We're

one of the best defensive teams in the league. Let's key on Payton in the second half and shut him down."

"That's right," agreed the linebacker. "Payton's no superstar. He doesn't have blazing speed. And he's not very big. He usually runs up the middle or on off-tackle slants. He tries to fool us with that short, stiff-legged stride. He darts into a hole and then cuts back and runs where we aren't ready for him. But we're the Vikings. We can stop him!"

The Vikings charged back out onto the field. They were determined to stop Walter Payton. On the first play, he got only 2 yards on a run over right tackle. But then he scampered around right end for 19 yards.

"All right, guys," said the Vikings' lineman. "I meant what I said before. We can stop Payton if we key on him."

The Bears called a draw play, but the Vikings weren't fooled. Walter got only 3 yards. A sweep around the end was followed by an off-tackle slant. The next two plays got the Bears nowhere. They had to punt.

When they had the ball again, the Bears turned once more to their star running back. But by now the Vikings were confident that they could stop Payton. The next time he was handed the ball, the Vikings' defense charged and nailed him for a 1-yard loss.

"Call my number again for a run around right end," Walter said to the quarterback back in the huddle.

The Bears couldn't believe their ears. Payton had spoken! But they weren't about to argue with the man who made their offense go. The quarterback called for a sweep around right end.

By the end of the play, Walter Payton had moved the ball 22 yards closer to the Vikings' goal line. Payton had sent a message: He would not be stopped this afternoon.

At the end of the third quarter, Walter Payton had carried the ball 34 times and

gained 192 yards. Along the Bears' bench players were whispering: "Could he do it? Could he break the single-game rushing record of 273 yards held by O. J. Simpson?"

With less than five minutes left in the game, Payton still needed 63 yards to match Simpson's record. The Chicago fans doubted he could do it. But the doubts disappeared as once more Payton charged off-tackle, cut to his right, and galloped down the sideline. After breaking two tackles with his straight-arm, he knocked over two other Vikings before stepping out of bounds. He had gained 58 yards on his longest run of the day. He had only gotten stronger—not tired—as the game went on.

A sweep around left end gained another 3 yards, giving Walter 271 yards for the day. There was time for one more carry. This time the sweep was to go around the right side. Reading his blocks and picking his way among players who were much taller and heavier, Payton gained another 4 yards. That made 275 yards. He broke the record and then some!

In just his third year in pro football, Walter Payton had broken the NFL's all-time single-game rushing record! What would he do next?

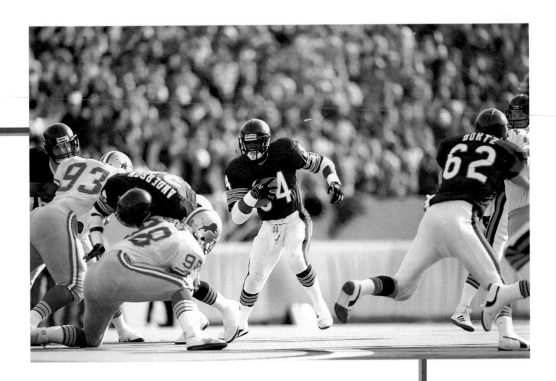

Walter Payton
(1954-   )

Before retiring after the 1987 season, Walter Payton did a lot more. He set many more NFL rushing records. On October 7, 1984, Walter broke Jim Brown's career rushing record, a record that had stood for 19 years!

But Walter Payton was a team player, and for much of his career, the Bears finished low in the standings. Then, finally, in 1986, Walter Payton received the one prize that he had always wanted: a Super Bowl ring! As he did during his football years, Mr. Payton gives a great deal of time to charities. He especially likes those causes that help children.

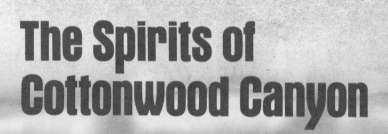

The Spirits of Cottonwood Canyon

"Hang on, Flournoy! We're almost there."

"Sandra!" shouted Flournoy, looking up to her cousin who was clinging to the rocks above her. "We should be getting home. I think it's getting kind of late."

Sandra, perched like a mountain goat on the rocks several feet ahead of Flournoy, looked out to the west. The sun was sinking low on the horizon. She knew that as the sun dipped behind the mountain, the sunset would come quickly here in Cottonwood Canyon in Arizona. Swiftly, figuring how much time they had before dark, Sandra yelled to her cousin below, "We have just a little farther to go. Come on, it's worth the climb!"

Sandra Day O'Connor became the first woman to serve on the Supreme Court of the United States.

Although Sandra was getting tired from the long climb, she hardly noticed. She kept scurrying up the rocks, being careful not to send a shower of stones down upon her cousin's head.

Both Sandra and Flournoy lived in the city of El Paso, Texas, during the school year, but Sandra's earliest memories were of this land of mountains and desert. Her grandfather had left Vermont and, in 1880, had settled in the desert land of Arizona. There, near the border of Mexico and just across the state line from New Mexico, Henry Clay Day started a cattle ranch. At that time, there were more native American Indians in the area than there were pioneer settlers.

Sandra's father now ran the ranch. He had taught Sandra to take good care of herself in the isolated wilderness of this 260-square-mile (673-square-kilometer) ranch.

According to the cowboys who worked the ranch, Sandra was a pretty fair cowgirl. From the time she was eight years old, she learned to help out with work on the ranch. Her father had taught her to brand cattle, mend fences, drive the ranch pickup truck and the tractor, and ride in the roundups. Sandra was even a good shot. She was expected to help on the ranch by shooting

jack rabbits, coyotes, and Gila monsters. Any animals that ate the pasture grass or endangered the cattle were fair game.

Sandra continued her climb up the rocks. In a few minutes she pulled herself up onto a ledge and announced, "I made it!"

She looked down below at Flournoy. "You're almost there now, just give me your hand," said Sandra, reaching to help Flournoy onto the ledge.

"Now what is it you were all fired up to show me?" asked Flournoy, looking around a little nervously. "Boy, this better be good."

Sandra had already moved across the ledge and was standing before a wall of rock. She gently ran her hand across the surface of the wall.

"Look, Flournoy, ancient Indian drawings! Just think how old they must be. I would guess they could be hundreds of years old—maybe even more."

Flournoy stepped closer to the wall and traced her finger over the carved drawings. "You were right, Sandra. This was worth the climb. I wonder what the drawings mean."

Sandra, who had learned a great deal about the Indians of Arizona, suggested, "Maybe these pictures tell stories of things that happened at that time—sort of an Indian newspaper. Or maybe they describe the adventures of an important Indian chief or warrior. You know, the Apaches used to live in this area. Some may even have had a hideout right here in this canyon. Doesn't it feel as if an Apache Indian could be hiding behind these rocks right now?"

Sandra was giving her cousin a devilish grin when they heard a howling sound echo through the canyon.

Flournoy looked startled for a moment and then in a whisper asked, "What was that?"

"I don't know, maybe it's an . . . Apache Indian spirit!" Sandra said laughingly.

"Don't worry, it's just a coyote. I guess we'd better get going. A lot of the creatures out here start moving around looking for food after dark."

Carefully, but quickly, the girls made their way down the rocks of the canyon wall. Soon, they were back on their horses and heading for home.

"Sandra!" Flournoy called out. "Do you think this is the right way? I'm afraid I don't remember which way we came. I hope we're not lost."

Sandra, sitting comfortably in the saddle of her horse, smiled and said, "Don't worry. I don't know exactly where we are either, but it's not too hard to figure out how to get home. See those fences up ahead?"

Flournoy looked out across the long stretch of dry scrub grass and cactuses. The setting sun caused long shadows to darken the ground. In the distance, she could barely see the lines of the pasture fences. To her, they were meaningless.

"I see them," Flournoy exclaimed. "But what good will those do us? They all look the same, and they seem to go on and on for miles."

"But each fence surrounds a different pasture," Sandra announced. "I've helped work on the fences all over this ranch. I'm sure I can tell which ones will lead us back home."

Flournoy looked doubtfully at her cousin but was comforted by her confidence.

Sandra nudged her horse and began to ride, yelling back to Flournoy, "Come on, let's go. I bet we'll be back home before supper's on the table!"

Sandra Day O'Connor
(1930-   )

The confidence and leadership Sandra showed that day in Cottonwood Canyon would help her in later life. Sandra grew up to become Justice Sandra Day O'Connor, the first woman appointed to the Supreme Court of the United States. Flournoy recalled the basis of this story in a published interview. Justice O'Connor says that this fictionalized account is similar to adventures she remembers growing up on the ranch.

Sandra graduated from law school at a time when very few women practiced as lawyers. She had trouble at first finding a job with a law firm because companies were not used to hiring women lawyers.

O'Connor proved herself a successful lawyer, however. Later, she entered politics in Arizona and eventually became a judge. In 1981, President Ronald Reagan chose her to serve on the highest court in our nation's government. There was little doubt that Sandra Day O'Connor could handle the job!

Run, Terry, Run

Greg Scott pedaled as hard as he could. His hands gripped the handlebars tightly. Beads of water formed on his forehead. But that didn't bother the ten-year-old rider a bit. The bright morning sun made Greg feel happy.

Greg liked the sound of his bicycle. *Zip 'n zip . . . zip 'n zip.* Sometimes Greg hummed along with the noise. Sometimes he made up funny rhymes with the sounds. "Zip 'n zip, I won't flip."

Greg's eyes were glued straight ahead. He had to be careful not to ride too close to the runner in front of him. Terry Fox, his muscles flexed, ran along the road ahead.

Terry Fox was a young athlete with bone cancer. His dream was to find a cure for the disease that left him with just one leg.

They had been moving together like this for two hours.

Terry looked back and smiled. "Hey, kid, how are you doing back there?" He called out to Greg often.

"Great, Terry, great!" Greg called out. "I'm not tired at all!"

Terry Fox and Greg Scott had many things in common. They both enjoyed being outdoors. They both loved baseball, basketball, soccer, and other sports. But the thing that brought them together this day was that both had lost a leg to bone cancer.

Skippety-hop, skippety-hop. Terry's legs made that sound on the highway. His left leg moved with a strong hop. His right leg was different. He had to use a skipping motion to move it. Terry's right leg was an artificial leg. It was made out of steel and fiberglass.

Everybody in Canada knew about Terry Fox. He was running across the country, about twenty-six miles (42 kilometers) a day. He wanted people to see that he was strong, even though he had an artificial leg.

When Terry and Greg first met, they talked about their disability. Greg's left leg was the artificial one. He showed Terry how he was able to ride a bicycle.

Terry told Greg, "I exercise for hours and hours—every day. I do pushups to build up my arm and shoulder muscles. And I walk and run to strengthen my good leg."

Greg chimed in, "Riding a bicycle makes me feel stronger. I'm learning how to be a good swimmer, too."

Now they were together, on a Canadian highway. Greg's parents had agreed to let him ride along with Terry for about six miles (9.7 kilometers). All along the way, people lined the road to wave to them.

Sometimes Terry would stop and give a speech. He asked people to donate money for cancer research.

"My dream is to find a cure for cancer. I believe in miracles. I want you to believe with me," Terry's voice was strong as he spoke. "A disability doesn't have to be a handicap." He wanted people who had lost arms or legs to know that just because they're disabled, it's not the end of their lives.

Terry Fox makes a stop to speak about his Marathon of Hope.

His message to other cancer patients was to never give up hoping for a cure. That's why his journey was called the Marathon of Hope.

Once he spoke to some schoolchildren. He liked to joke. "I bet you feel sorry for me. Well, you don't have to. I've broken my artificial knee several times and it doesn't hurt a bit!"

Greg joined Terry on the 138th day of the run. Whenever Terry ran, the people of Canada came out to greet him. They waved and cheered. Some people cried, too. Radio and television stations sent out reporters and camera crews to follow him. Somebody even wrote a song. The song was called "Run, Terry, Run."

Zip 'n zip, zip 'n zip. Skippety-hop, skippety-hop. Greg and Terry moved

steadily along the Canadian highway.

"Hey, Greg, how're we doing? We've gone about three miles already. Ready for a break?" Terry called out, as he turned around to smile at the boy behind him.

"Anytime is okay with me!" Greg yelled happily. His pedaling slowed down. "It looks like the van is waiting up ahead."

Two young men rode ahead of Terry and Greg in a van. At the end of each mile (1.6 kilometers), they pulled over to the side of the road. When Terry caught up with them, they would have water and a snack ready, in case he wanted to rest.

The driver of the van stepped out smiling. He was Terry's school friend, Doug Alward. Darrell Fox, Terry's younger brother, was riding in the van too. He cheerfully handed out water and towels.

Then all four of them stretched out on a grassy patch of ground. Darrell passed around snacks to eat.

Greg quietly walked away from the group. He took off his hat to cool off. There was no hair on his head. He was bald. Terry walked over to him and spoke gently. "After some of the cancer treatments, my hair fell out, too." Terry pointed to his own thick, brown curls. "Someday yours will look like this."

Terry put his hand around Greg's shoulder. "Losing my hair made me almost as angry as losing my leg. But I decided that nobody is ever going to call me a quitter."

"After this operation," Terry said, "I made up my mind about life. Being sad would never make me well. I cheered up whenever I thought about sports I love. I thought about my family and friends. I didn't want to disappoint them. And I didn't want to let down the people in the hospital. My doctors and nurses—and the eight buddies in my ward—they were all cheering for me."

Greg and Terry walked back to the others. They walked tall, proudly displaying their T-shirts. Marathon of Hope was printed on the front of Terry's. Under those bold letters was a map of Canada. The country's national symbol, a maple leaf, was in the center. Greg's shirt had the same picture. Around it were written the words *Terry Fox Ten Million Dollar Run.*

It was time to continue the journey. Doug and Darrell climbed into the van. They pulled onto the highway and began to drive slowly. Next, Terry began to run. Then Greg fixed his hat firmly on his head. He mounted his bicycle and began to pedal.

"Skippety-hop, we'll never stop. Zip 'n zip, what a great trip." The ten-year-old began to hum. His heart was filled with hope. His eyes were fixed on Terry Fox.

Terry Fox
(1958-1981)

Terry Fox was born in Winnipeg, Manitoba, Canada. When he was eighteen, in 1977, he lost his right leg to cancer. After the operation, Terry worked hard to become strong. He became active in many sports, including golf and wheelchair basketball, and he began running every day. In 1980, he began his run across Canada. He made speeches and asked people to give money to fight cancer. Terry ran 3,339 miles (5,374 kilometers). His run raised about $25 million for cancer research and won him great honor from the Canadian government. He was forced to stop when the cancer spread. The "Terry Fox Run" is still held today in honor of this courageous young athlete. Terry Fox died in 1981.

Jane Goodall helps animals. She taught the world about chimpanzees in Africa.

A Forest Home

The rain pelted down heavily as Jane hurried through the forest. Suddenly she froze, almost afraid to breathe. Right there, hunched in front of her, was a large chimpanzee. She knew that if she upset or scared the animal, he could be very dangerous.

A sound rustled above. Jane looked up to see another big chimp. He looked right at her and screamed *WRAAAAH*. This is a chimp's way of threatening a dangerous animal. Branches started shaking all around

The Joy and Fun of Books

Beverly Cleary created the stories about Ramona Quimby, Henry Huggins, Ribsy, and Ralph. She writes honest, funny books about everyday life.

She encouraged her students to use imagination in their writing. Once the class was to pretend they lived in George Washington's time and write about an experience. Another assignment was writing about a favorite book character. Miss Smith was so pleased with the work Beverly turned in, she told the class: "When Beverly grows up, she should write children's books."

"Someday," Beverly thought, "I'll write books that will make kids laugh. And maybe my books will end up on the shelves of their library."

The teacher's prediction certainly came true! First came high school and college, though. Then Beverly decided to be a librarian, with a special interest in children's books. The joy of reading was something she wanted every child to experience. When offered a children's librarian job in Yakima, Washington, Beverly happily accepted.

School groups often visited her library. One group of boys was always complaining that books were too hard, too easy, or boring. They couldn't find books that were fun to read. Several years later, Beverly Cleary had those boys in mind when she wrote her first book of stories, *Henry Huggins*. She wanted Henry to be an average boy. He would live on Klickitat Street, in the same neighborhood that Beverly had lived in

Portland. His friends would include a girl with the nickname of Beezus, who happened to have a pesty little sister named Ramona.

The stories about Henry expanded to more books about children with real-life experiences. *Ellen Tebbits*, like young Beverly, worried that others would find out about the old-fashioned woolen underwear her mother made her wear. *Otis Spofford* ruined a school fiesta by "turning the tables" on the bullfighter. Otis played the front half of a bull in a school program and ruined the whole program.

Animals play important parts in Beverly Cleary's stories, too. One day a stray dog named Ribsy followed Henry Huggins. Since Henry could not resist the scruffy dog, he scrunched him into a shopping bag and took him home on the bus.

Then there's *Ralph S. Mouse*, one of literature's lovable mice. Ralph was "born" after Beverly's son had to spend time in bed with a fever. The Cleary family was on vacation. To keep her son busy in the hotel room, Beverly bought small toy cars and a tiny motorcycle. The little boy raced them across the stripes of the bedspread. Back at home, a neighbor showed Beverly how a tiny mouse had fallen into a pail and couldn't get out. Cleary combined the two images, and Ralph came to life in *The Mouse and the Motorcycle*.

When her twins were about eleven years old, the author wrote *Mitch and Amy*, about the year when they were in fourth grade. The story is about normal brother-and-sister problems, like squabbling over who gets to send away for the cereal-box offer. Although the twins had spats, they often came to one another's rescue. When Mitchell—like Beverly's son—couldn't find books that interested him, his sister Amy—like Beverly's daughter—helped with that problem.

When she finished *Mitch and Amy*, Beverly asked for her children's comments.

Marianne said, "I love it, love it, love it!"

Malcolm said, "Make it a thousand pages!"

Beverly Cleary
(1916-   )

Beverly Cleary has written more than thirty books for young readers. Her first book of stories, *Henry Huggins*, was published in 1950. *Ramona and Her Father* and *Ramona Quimby, Age 8* were Newbery Honor Books. *Dear Mr. Henshaw* won the Newbery Medal. Other books have brought her awards and special honors, many of them based on the votes of her readers.

Buildings That Serve People

Imagine that you receive a huge box full of blocks. What will you build with them? A house? A castle? A shopping mall? A skyscraper?

Whatever you build, you are acting as an architect. Architects are people who design buildings of all types. They draw the plans, select the materials, and oversee the builders. Today, there are many architects in the United States. One of the best is I. M. Pei (pay).

What makes an architect great? It is his or her ability to create new ideas for what must be done. The architect has to make a building

I. M. Pei is one of the best architects in the United States. He wants his buildings to be friendly to the people they serve.

Workers confer on the "ground floor,"
building the Fragrant Hill Hotel in Beijing
(above). The triangular court of the
National Gallery dazzles the eye (center).

that will be just right for its location and
the people using it.

Sometimes an architect will use
materials in a new, startling way. Mr. Pei
likes to use concrete and glass. One of his
most talked-about designs is a pyramid of
glass. It stands in the courtyard of the
Louvre (LOO vruh), a famous art museum
in Paris, France. There it makes up the
entrance to new paths into the museum.

An architect may find a striking way to
solve problems of space. I. M.'s design for
the John F. Kennedy Library in Boston,
Massachusetts, had to fit a small site. "Yet
the building cannot give the appearance of
being small," Pei said. "It represents not just

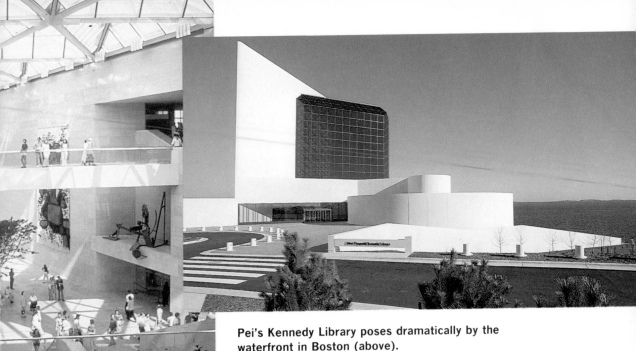

Pei's Kennedy Library poses dramatically by the waterfront in Boston (above).

Kennedy himself, but the importance of the presidency during the years when Kennedy was President." He solved the problem with a building that unites three shapes made of concrete and glass—a cube, a cylinder, and a tall triangle.

Mr. Pei faced a different problem in designing the Fragrant Hill Hotel outside Beijing (bay jihng), China. (Beijing is also known as Peking.) There he wanted to combine Chinese tradition with modern styles. The result is a building that is both traditional and modern. For example, it has walls made of Chinese stucco (a kind of plaster) and tile, and the lobby roof is made of glass and metal.

I. M. is an energetic, friendly man. He wants his buildings, too, to be friendly, both to their users and to their neighborhoods. "Buildings," he says, "are here to serve, and they must solve the problem of serving well."

I. M. was born in Guangzhou (gwahng joh), China, in 1917. (Guangzhou was once known as Canton.) His father was an official with the Bank of China. Young Pei grew up in Hong Kong and Shanghai. In high school in Shanghai, he became fascinated by the new buildings going up throughout the city. Soon he knew he wanted to be involved in architecture. Going to college in America would be the place to start.

In 1935, at the age of eighteen, Mr. Pei came to the United States. American students couldn't pronounce his Chinese name, which is Ieoh Ming. They used his initials instead, and so has everyone else. Pei intended to study architecture. But before classes started, he discovered that architecture students had to draw pictures of their buildings. He didn't think he could draw. So he decided to study engineering, the science of designing structures, machines, and other products, at Massachusetts Institute of Technology. Later, he was persuaded to return to architecture. In 1940, he graduated from MIT with a degree in architecture.

By then, a great war known as World War II had begun. Mr. Pei decided to wait in the United States for the war to end. He volunteered for service with the National Defense Research Committee, a group that coordinated science projects for the war. In 1942, he married Eileen Loo. She, too, was Chinese-born and attended college in the United States.

When Eileen enrolled at Harvard to study landscape architecture, I. M. met some of Harvard's architecture professors. With their encouragement, he continued his studies at the Graduate School of Design.

"The Harvard time was wonderful," I. M. says. The head of the architecture department was Walter Gropius (GROH pee uhs). Before leaving Germany, Gropius had been his country's most important architect.

Pei and an associate discuss a project (left). A sketch drawn by I. M. (below) shows his design idea for the East Building of the National Gallery of Art.

Pei has always remembered what a great teacher he was.

After graduating in 1946, Pei hoped to return home, but his father advised him that China was in chaos. So he became a teacher at Harvard instead. Two years later, he became director of architecture for a major company. The company's projects included everything from housing projects to skyscrapers. On this job, I. M. learned about the need to satisfy all the people connected with a building—those who pay for it, those who use it, and those in the neighborhood who see it.

Eventually Pei realized he could not leave the country he had become so used to. He became an American citizen in 1954.

The following year the architect and several friends from his Harvard days founded a firm now known as I. M. Pei & Partners. The Paris pyramid, the Kennedy Library, and the Beijing hotel are only 3 of more than 100 projects the firm has completed. Altogether,

Pei's Mesa Laboratory in Colorado was designed to blend with its surroundings.

these projects have received about 100 awards.

Perhaps the firm's best-known building in the United States is the East Building of the National Gallery of Art in Washington, D.C. The East Building is made up of two triangular buildings. In the middle of the two is an enormous triangular court with a glass roof. Inside the court, ramps and stairs hug the white walls. White bridges leap across from one side to another. Visitors find the room as exciting as the art hung on its walls. They enjoy climbing the stairs and crossing the bridges just as if they were on a jungle gym.

One observer called the building as a whole "one giant jigsaw puzzle." Another added that it is "a public delight and a city's pride." I. M. Pei himself is proud that his building has proved to be so friendly.

I. M. Pei
(1917-   )

I. M. Pei is widely recognized as one of the top architects in the United States. He lives in New York City with his wife, Eileen. They have three sons and a daughter; two of the sons are architects with their father's firm, I. M. Pei & Partners.

Mother of the Poor

Mother Teresa cares about the sick and homeless poor in India. She also does something to help them.

Mother Teresa hardly felt the blazing sun beat down upon her shoulders. She noticed something in the road up ahead. A woman lay in the gutter along the roadside. She watched as people passed the woman by. Rushing toward the woman, Mother Teresa knelt beside her on the filthy ground.

"My friend, where is your home? I will take you there."

Mother Teresa had to strain to hear her reply.

"I have no home."

The woman lay in the dirt, too sick and weak to move. She was dying.

"I must get you to a hospital." Mother Teresa said. "You are ill and need help."

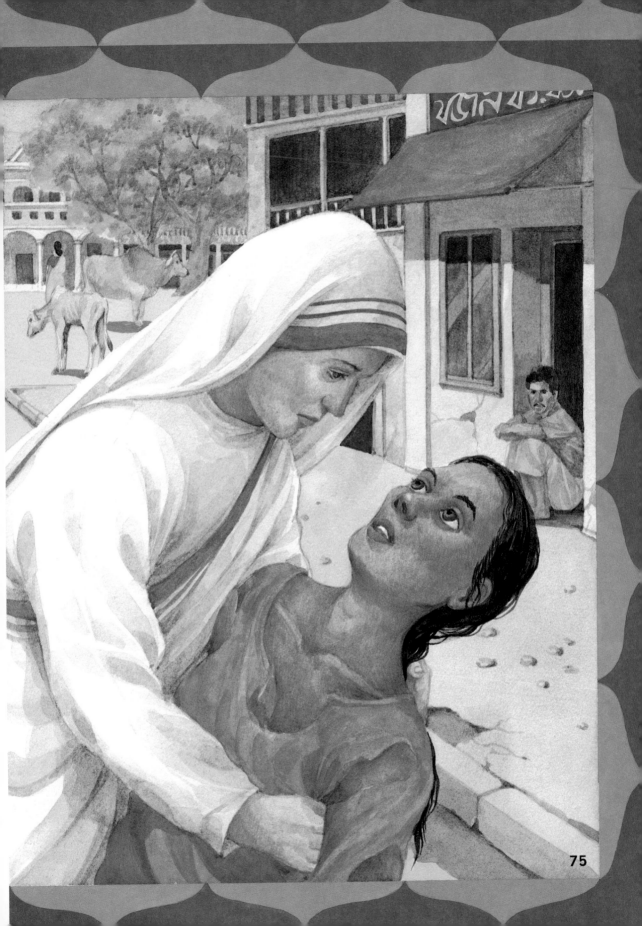

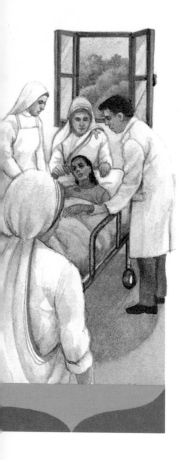

The people of Calcutta, India, often saw this tiny Catholic nun walking through the city's slums. As Mother Teresa knelt beside the dying woman, her usually smiling face showed anger.

"Why must this person lie in the street, ignored and uncared for?" she asked herself.

Mother Teresa took the woman to a nearby hospital and stayed until the hospital agreed to care for her. As she left, Mother Teresa prayed for the unknown woman who would now die in the hospital. But her prayers did not relieve her anger.

"These people should not have to die in the street like animals!" she thought.

Every day, Mother Teresa saw people dying in the streets of Calcutta. It was 1952 then, and thousands of people were homeless in India. These people had no one to care for them when they were sick and hungry. That's why she had come here.

In 1928, Mother Teresa became a nun and began to devote her life to the Catholic Church. She joined a convent, a place where nuns live, in India. Years later she was given permission to leave the convent so she could work with the poor people of Calcutta. She hoped to open a home for the dying. There she could love and care for these people. The "poorest of the poor," she called them.

After leaving the dying woman at the hospital, Mother Teresa set out for city hall.

"Why must people in this city die in the streets like dogs?" she asked the city officials. The small woman's sharp words surprised them. But the officials agreed with her that the dying needed care and shelter. Soon, they decided on a place where Mother Teresa could take them—a Hindu temple. Most people in India practice the Hindu religion. A temple is a special place of worship.

Mother Teresa was allowed to use a small building behind the temple. Although the rooms were filthy, Mother Teresa thanked God for her good fortune. She named the home *Nirmal Hriday*, which means "the Place of the Pure Heart." Next, she brought in other nuns, called sisters, to work with

Mother Teresa set up her hospital on the grounds of this temple, here on a busy street in Calcutta.

her. Together they scrubbed the walls and floors of the building.

"Mother Teresa," asked one sister, "where will we put these poor people? We have no beds."

"They will rest on the floor for now," Mother Teresa answered. "It is better than the mud and the dirt in the street."

So the sisters went out into the street and brought the sick into *Nirmal Hriday*. As the home began to fill up with people, the neighbors became angry. The sisters' home was not in the temple itself. But it was on

the holy temple's grounds and it was
attached to the temple.

One day, a crowd gathered in front of the
home. "Get out! These people soil our holy
temple. This is a Hindu temple, not a
Catholic church!" a man shouted.

He picked up a stone and threw it at the
sisters who were leaving the home. Others
picked up sticks and stones, and flung them
at the sisters, forcing them back into the
building.

"Mother Teresa! What can we do?" the
sisters cried.

"We must pray for their understanding," Mother Teresa answered. Then there was a knock at the door. The door opened suddenly and in walked the police commissioner.

"Mother Teresa," he began seriously, "this is a Hindu temple and it is sacred to the Hindu people. The people outside believe that you are trying to convert these people to your religion. They demand that you leave."

"I assure you, sir, we wish only to comfort these people," the nun replied firmly. "They have nowhere else to go. You are most welcome to watch us work. As you can see, we are very busy."

Mother Teresa then turned briskly and said, "Continue, sisters. We have much to do."

Mother Teresa and the sisters went back to their work of tending to the sick. The police commissioner who stood watching her then looked around. Each of the sisters was bathing, bandaging, or giving medicine to one of the sick and dying people. He left, quietly closing the door behind him.

Through an open window, Mother Teresa heard angry cries as the commissioner met the crowd outside the door.

"Why have you not forced those women to leave?" someone called out.

Others joined in, shouting angrily.

"I want you all to go home," he announced. "Then I want you to ask your sisters and your mothers to return to the temple. Tell them to do what these nuns are doing. Ask them to wash the sores of the sick, to bandage their wounds, and to give these poor people love and kindness. If they do these things, I will force the Catholic sisters to leave. Until then, the sisters can stay and continue their work."

Mother Teresa
(1910-   )

Mother Teresa founded the Missionaries of Charity, a religious organization that cares for the needy in many countries. For her tireless work with the poor, she was awarded the Nobel Peace Prize in 1979. Nobel Prize winners are people who have helped the world become a better place through their work.

Mother Teresa grew up in an area that now is part of Yugoslavia. Inspired by stories she read and heard about the missionaries in India, she became a nun and began to serve the "poorest of the poor" in India. She teaches them. She gives them food and shelter. But, more than anything, she gives them love.

Rosa Parks needed a seat on the bus one day in 1955. Her actions that day led the bus company to treat black riders more fairly.

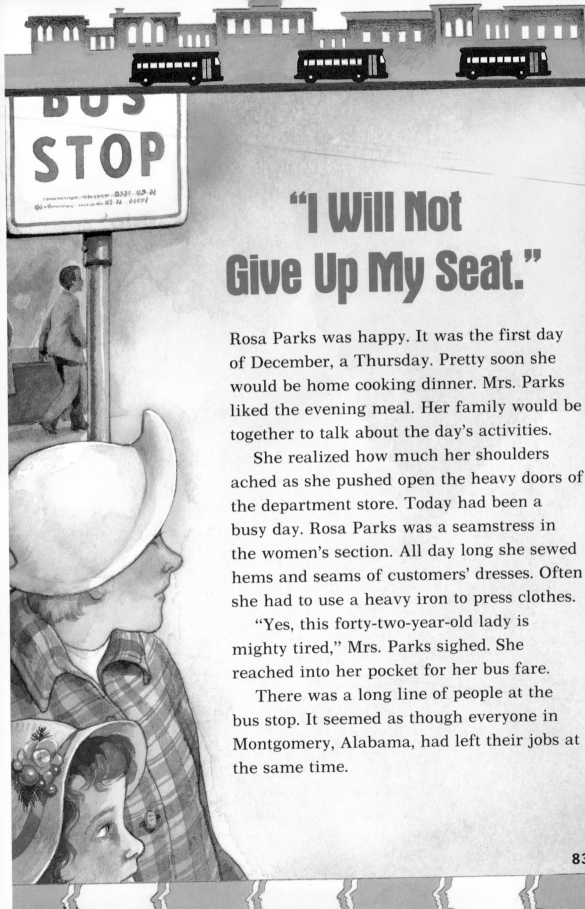

"I Will Not Give Up My Seat."

Rosa Parks was happy. It was the first day of December, a Thursday. Pretty soon she would be home cooking dinner. Mrs. Parks liked the evening meal. Her family would be together to talk about the day's activities.

She realized how much her shoulders ached as she pushed open the heavy doors of the department store. Today had been a busy day. Rosa Parks was a seamstress in the women's section. All day long she sewed hems and seams of customers' dresses. Often she had to use a heavy iron to press clothes.

"Yes, this forty-two-year-old lady is mighty tired," Mrs. Parks sighed. She reached into her pocket for her bus fare.

There was a long line of people at the bus stop. It seemed as though everyone in Montgomery, Alabama, had left their jobs at the same time.

"Here comes the Cleveland Avenue bus!" somebody called out. That was the bus Rosa Parks usually took home. But as she moved closer to the front of the line, she saw that the bus was almost full.

A few seats were empty at the front of the bus. The back was filled with passengers. "What's the use getting on," she thought. "Black people can't sit in those front seats, anyway. Only white people can use them."

Rosa Parks didn't feel like standing all the way home. The pain in her shoulders was getting worse. Her feet hurt, too. So she decided to wait for another bus.

Not long after the first bus left, another one pulled up. There were plenty of seats on it. Mrs. Parks stepped aboard and paid her fare. She chose a seat in the middle, in the first row of the black people's section.

"It feels so good to sit down," she thought. Her shoulders still ached, but at least her feet felt better. She adjusted her eyeglasses and sat back to relax.

Rosa's eyes turned to the scenes outside. Holiday decorations were displayed in the stores. She was so busy looking out that she did not notice that the bus had filled up. A white man walked down the aisle looking for a seat. But there were no empty seats.

The bus company had a rule back in those days. If there were no empty seats for white passengers in the middle section, the black passengers in those seats had to move.

The driver turned to speak to the black people in the middle section. "You all better stand and give up those seats."

Three other people in Mrs. Parks's row stood up. They walked to the back of the bus. Rosa Parks did not budge.

Angrily, the driver got up and walked over to face her. "Didn't you hear me say to get up? You know the rules!"

Rosa Parks closed her eyes for a moment. She thought about her aching shoulders. She thought about how tired her feet were. But most of all, she thought how unfair it was that she was being forced to give up her seat.

Taking a deep breath, Mrs. Parks replied, "Yes, I heard what you said. But no, I will not give up my seat." She had made up her mind. She was tired of rules that were unfair.

The driver became more angry. He was supposed to follow company rules. "I'm telling you to get up out of that seat or I'll have you arrested!"

The passenger felt strong, and she spoke firmly. "Go ahead and have me arrested. I will not give up my seat." The bus driver stomped off to call the police. "Let the law deal with her," he muttered.

Other passengers looked at the determined passenger with surprise. Mrs. Parks was a small woman, properly dressed. Her hair was brushed back neatly. She didn't look like a person who would be outspoken.

Rosa Parks sat up straight and calmly stared out the window. Soon a policeman boarded the bus. He walked over to question her. "Didn't the driver tell you to give up that seat? Why didn't you stand up?"

"Because I don't think I should have
to. I paid my fare, just like everybody else."
Then she asked him quietly, "Why do you
push us around?"

The policeman replied, "The law is the
law. I must arrest you." He walked Mrs.
Parks off the bus to a waiting police car.
She was driven directly to the Montgomery
police station.

Rosa Parks, walking tall and proud, was led into the station. Her fingerprints were taken and she was charged with not obeying the laws. A policeman led her into a small jail cell. She closed her eyes to rest, determined not to be frightened. Her grandparents had been slaves. They had survived beatings and insults. Certainly she could endure this.

Rosa Parks thought about herself. There comes a time when people must speak out. *And the time for me is now!* Maybe other black folks will hear about what is happening in Montgomery, Alabama. Maybe they will decide to speak out, too.

Some black people had been talking about a bus boycott. This meant that they would refuse to ride the buses if they were expected to give up their seats. They would walk or use cars to get places. Without fares from black bus riders, the bus company would lose money.

A business can't last long if it's losing money, Mrs. Parks knew. "Maybe it will take a boycott or something like that to make our city care about all of its citizens," she thought.

Rosa Parks opened her eyes. She saw that some friends had arrived. They had paid some bail money to get her out of jail. A judge would hear the case in a few days.

"Thank you for coming to my aid," she said, smiling. "I hope everybody will understand why I was put in jail. The black citizens of Montgomery must demand to be heard. Let us all agree not to ride the buses until we are treated fairly!"

Rosa Parks takes a seat on the bus in 1956. One year earlier, it might have been against the law for her to take a seat on a crowded bus.

Rosa Parks
(1913-)

Rosa Parks became known all over the world. Because of her brave actions, other people gained the courage to speak out for fair treatment. The Montgomery bus boycott began that year, 1955, and lasted for 382 days. Finally, the Supreme Court of the United States decided that the bus company had to change its rules. Black people and white people must be treated equally. In the years that followed, there were many other activities that led to fairer treatment of black Americans.

Rosa Parks kept on speaking out for equal rights. She continued her work in the Montgomery Voters League. That group worked to encourage people to vote. She later worked as an aide to a member of Congress, and founded the Rosa and Raymond Parks Institute. This is an organization that helps children achieve their best.

Roberto Clemente was
the first Latin American
to be elected to the
Baseball Hall of Fame.

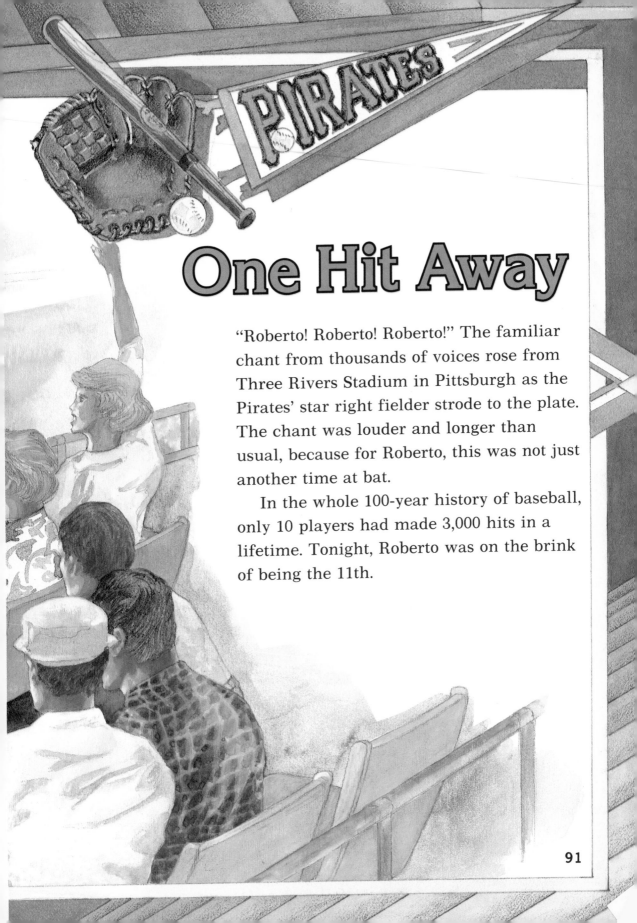

One Hit Away

"Roberto! Roberto! Roberto!" The familiar chant from thousands of voices rose from Three Rivers Stadium in Pittsburgh as the Pirates' star right fielder strode to the plate. The chant was louder and longer than usual, because for Roberto, this was not just another time at bat.

In the whole 100-year history of baseball, only 10 players had made 3,000 hits in a lifetime. Tonight, Roberto was on the brink of being the 11th.

The 1972 season had started with Roberto only about 100 hits away from the prized 3,000. Number 2,999 had come in Philadelphia the night before, September 28. Roberto had taken himself out of the game after that so he could try for the big one in Pittsburgh, before a hometown crowd.

Now it was the Mets, with their great pitcher, Tom Seaver, on the mound.

"Seaver's looking for win number 20," a teammate said to Roberto before the game. "It'll give him two 20-win seasons in a row."

"I know," Roberto said.

"He'll be tough tonight."

"Seaver's always tough," Roberto replied.

Facing Roberto in the first inning, Seaver reared back and threw. Roberto hit the ball, but not well. Skipping over Seaver's glove, it bounced toward second base. The Mets' second baseman moved quickly to his right, scooped the ball, and threw to first. Roberto charged down the base line and beat it out.

The scoreboard flashed "H," meaning Roberto had made a hit, and there it was: a blooper, but number 3,000, the end of a long quest, the crown of 18 seasons in the majors.

	1	2	3	4	5	6	7	8	9	R	H	E
METS	0									0	0	1
PIRATES										0	0	0

The crowd went wild, shouting "Roberto!" "He's done it!" "He made it!"

He had not. The scoreboard had only blinked "H" before the official scorer had changed it to "E." "Error, second baseman," boomed out of the loudspeaker.

Roberto did not object. "I really didn't want the hit like that anyway," he said. He still had at least three more times at bat.

That did not help. Three more times at bat proved to be only three more outs.

Roberto had begun playing ball back home in Puerto Rico when he was hardly big enough to swing a bat. Mainly he played softball, but sometimes he would play sandlot baseball. He played ball first thing in the morning, last thing at night, and all the time in between. "I would forget to eat because of baseball," he told a friend once.

As a Pirate, Roberto was a great success. He made impossible catches in the outfield.

His throws, even from near the fence, were swift and accurate. At bat, he was fearsome. He hit better than .300 in each of 13 seasons. His best was in 1961, when he led the National League with .351. He set a record for 10 hits in 2 consecutive games.

"I'm tired," Roberto said as he sat in the locker room after going 0 for 4 against the Mets. The ache that had bothered his neck and shoulders for so long was worse. He had played in 2,432 big-league games. He had been at bat 9,452 times. The National

League play-offs between Pittsburgh and Cincinnati were only days away. "I need a rest to get ready for the play-offs," Roberto said. "If I don't get that hit this weekend, I'll just wait until next year."

On the night of September 30, Roberto came up in the first inning against the Mets' fireballing pitcher, Jon Matlack. Roberto struck out.

The crowd was silent. It looked like this game would be a repeat of the night before.

"Go get it," his teammate Willie Stargell said as he handed Roberto his bat in the fourth inning. Roberto kept his usual *cara de palo*—the "wooden face" he wore in public—as he walked slowly to the plate. There he crouched, and cocked his bat.

Roberto did not move as Matlack's first pitch went by. A strike. He dug deeper in the batter's box.

"Hit it out of the park, Roberto!" a lonely voice yelled from the stands. But no cheers followed. The crowd sat hushed, waiting.

Matlack chunked the ball into his glove a couple of times, tugged at the bill of his cap, and wound up. The second pitch was just what Roberto wanted, and he swung. As he followed through, he could see the ball taking off on a terrific line drive toward the fence in left center field. It hit the fence and bounced back. Roberto sped to second base.

Noise now burst out of Three Rivers Stadium as never before. Cheers, shouts, handclaps, and whistles went on for more than a full minute as Roberto stood on second base doffing his cap. The umpire hustled over, shook Roberto's hand, and gave him the ball.

Roberto played one more inning, then left the game. "For an 'old man,'" the thirty-eight-year-old superstar realized happily, "I haven't had a bad year!" After the play-offs, though, there would be no more hits for Roberto.

December found Roberto in Puerto Rico, where he always spent the winter. An earthquake had struck Nicaragua, a country in Central America. Its capital, Managua, was in ruins. Thousands of people there needed food and shelter desperately. Roberto wanted to help. He decided to take some supplies to Nicaragua. On New Year's Eve, Roberto and others sat in an old, heavily loaded cargo plane as it struggled off the ground, banked to the left, and crashed into the Atlantic Ocean. There were no survivors.

On New Year's Day, 1973, Puerto Rico's new governor, Rafael Hernández Colón, was sworn into office. After a minute of silence to honor Roberto, the governor said, "Our people have lost one of their glories. All our hearts are saddened . . ."

BASEBALL'S GREATEST

★ ★

HITTERS ROBERTO CLEMENTE

BASEBALL'S GREATEST
HITTERS

★ ROBERTO
CLEMENTE OF
PITTSBURGH PIRATES
HT. 5-11 WT. 175 B.8-18-34 D. 12-31-72
Bats-R Throws-R

Considered to be the best player ever to come out of Purto Rico, Roberto won four National League batting titles during an 18-year career (1955-72) that was spent entirely with the Pirates. He hit over .300 in a season 13 times, achieving a career high of .357 in 1967. Roberto led the league in hits twice, in triples once and was named the league's Most Valuable Player in 1966. A member of the Hall of Fame, he is one of 14 players to collect 3,000 career hits.

G	AB	R	H	BA	HR	RBI
2433	9454	1416	3000	.317	240	1305

© TCMA Ltd. 1982-4

Roberto Clemente

(1934-1972)

Roberto Clemente was one of history's greatest baseball players. Three months after his death, he was the first Latin American to be elected to the Baseball Hall of Fame. He won four National League batting titles and had a lifetime average of .317. Clemente won the National League's Most Valuable Player award in 1966. He played in 12 All-Star games and helped the Pirates to victories in the World Series of 1960 and 1971, hitting .310 in one and .414 in the other.

Golda Meir wanted Jews
to have a land they could
call their own.

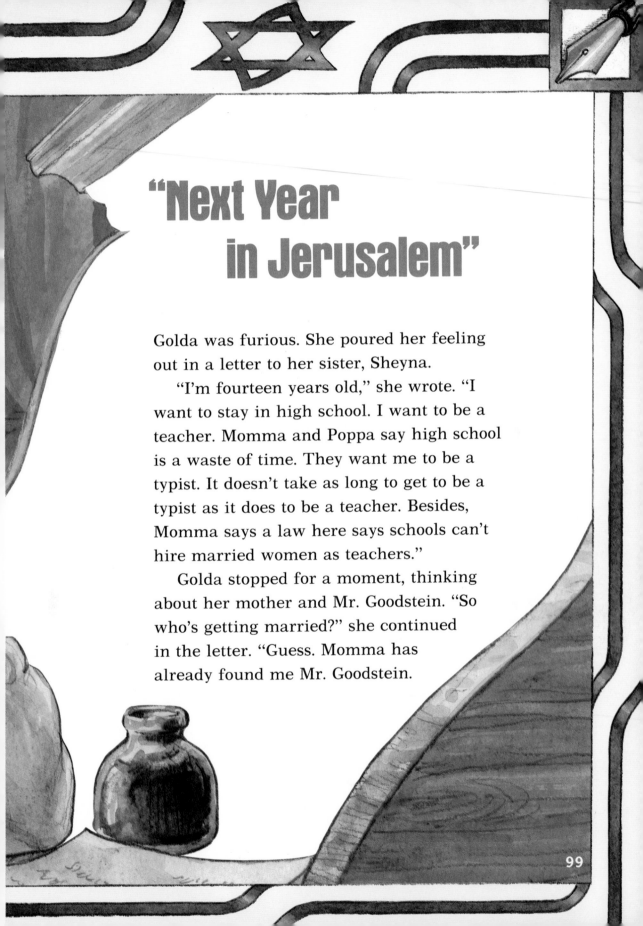

"Next Year in Jerusalem"

Golda was furious. She poured her feeling out in a letter to her sister, Sheyna.

"I'm fourteen years old," she wrote. "I want to stay in high school. I want to be a teacher. Momma and Poppa say high school is a waste of time. They want me to be a typist. It doesn't take as long to get to be a typist as it does to be a teacher. Besides, Momma says a law here says schools can't hire married women as teachers."

Golda stopped for a moment, thinking about her mother and Mr. Goodstein. "So who's getting married?" she continued in the letter. "Guess. Momma has already found me Mr. Goodstein.

He's more than thirty years old—an old man! He says he'll wait until I'm older. He'll wait all right—*forever* as far as I'm concerned."

It was 1912 in Milwaukee, Wisconsin, and Golda's parents kept to the old ways. In Jewish families it had long been the custom for parents to choose husbands for their daughters. Certain other groups of people had the same custom. Parents believed that they could make wise choices for their daughters. And besides, it was always done that way.

Customs change, though. Even in Golda's time, more Jewish daughters were deciding whom they would marry.

"And as for our grocery store," Golda went on in her letter, "I have to be there before school and after school. In the morning, Momma goes to the produce market to buy things to sell. Often she doesn't get back until after school starts, and I'm late. My teachers don't like that."

Golda ended her letter, "What can I do, Sheyna? What can I do?"

An answer came quickly. It came from Shamai, Sheyna's husband. "Come to us," the letter said. "Leave Milwaukee and live in Denver. You can go to school here. Just tell us when you're coming."

Leaving home would not be easy, though. First, Golda needed money for a train ticket to Denver. Sheyna sent her some, but the ticket cost more than that. Second, her parents would not want her to go.

Golda talked about money with her friends, Regina and Sarah. Sarah loaned Golda some money. Regina and Golda came up with a plan to earn money. "Well," Regina said, "both our families came to America when we were young. We didn't know English, but we learned it quickly." Golda agreed. She had come to America from Russia when she was eight years old. Now she spoke English perfectly.

"Here in Milwaukee," Regina went on, "there are lots of people from other countries who don't know English." Regina and Golda decided to give English lessons. They charged ten cents an hour.

"Regina and Sarah, you are good friends," said Golda.

Regina and Golda found some students, and they began to earn their ten cents an hour. Months passed, but slowly the dimes added up. Golda finally had enough money to buy a train ticket.

Golda's mother had not been happy with Golda's attitude toward Mr. Goodstein. And neither of her parents would be able to accept Golda's going off to Denver. "Education is wasted on girls, Golda," her father would say again and again. "If you must go to school, fine. But be a typist, please. But all you really need to do is settle down with a husband."

"And besides," her mother would join in, "right now I need you in the grocery store." They were a loving family, but father, mother, and daughter argued endlessly over Golda's future.

Golda was determined, though. "I want to be a teacher," she told them. "And I think I can be the best teacher in the world. But I must go to school." Even if it means going away for at least a while, Golda thought.

At last, the time to leave Milwaukee came. Golda poured out her feelings one more time to her parents, in a note. She told them not to worry, that she would be safe. The next morning she went to the train station and bought a ticket for Denver. The

journey took about two days. Sheyna and
Shamai were at the Denver station to
welcome her.

Golda went to school in Denver. She also
spent many hours listening to young men
and women who often came to Sheyna and
Shamai's house to talk. And what they
talked a lot about was Palestine (PAL ih
styn), a small land at the eastern end of the
Mediterranean Sea.

Many hundreds of years ago, Palestine
had been a Jewish land. Jerusalem was a
holy city there. Then people called Romans
conquered Palestine. They forced the Jews to
leave. Eventually, most Jews became

scattered all over the world. They had no homeland of their own. Through the years, Palestine was ruled by other nations.

But now, the time of Golda's girlhood, Jews were moving back to Palestine. Thousands of others wanted to move there. They also wanted Palestine to become a separate nation. The young people to whom Golda listened were among those who wanted that.

Each year at the Passover feast, Jews raised glasses of wine and said, "Next year in Jerusalem." But years passed and nothing happened. More Jews came to Palestine, but it was not a separate nation.

Golda had gone to Denver with one idea in mind, to go to school and become a teacher. In Denver, as she talked with Jews about Palestine and studied and read more about her people, she began to find another goal—to make "next year in Jerusalem" come true.

Over the years, Golda often thought about that letter from Shamai, inviting her to come to Denver. "That letter was a turning point in my life because it was in Denver that my real education began," she said. "Shamai's offer was like a lifeline and I grabbed it."

Golda Meir
(1898-1978)

Golda and her parents made peace with each other during her absence. Then she returned to Milwaukee for a time, at their request. In 1921, when she was twenty-three years old, she left America to live in Palestine. More than anything, Golda wanted to help build Palestine into a homeland for Jews of the world. In 1948, her dream came true. Palestine became the new nation of Israel. Golda took part in the government. Then, in 1969, she became Israel's prime minister, the head of government. Golda Meir lived to be eighty years old.

Percy Julian made people's lives better through medicine.

The Soybean Chemist

The six Julian children of Montgomery, Alabama, were lucky. Like all parents, Mr. and Mrs. Julian wanted their children to be healthy and happy. Percy Julian's parents wanted their children to set high goals in life, too.

All six children were sent to college, which was unusual in the 1920's and 1930's. Percy's sisters became successful in teaching and social work. His two brothers became doctors. When the time came for Percy to choose a career, his father encouraged him to become a doctor.

Percy certainly liked the idea of studying medicine, but he had another idea. "There are other ways of helping people who are sick. I would rather be a chemist. Maybe I can discover medicines that will keep people well," he suggested to his father.

Mr. and Mrs. Julian agreed that their son should choose a career that he liked. So Percy studied chemistry in college. Chemistry is a science. Chemists study the substances that make up the universe. Percy was a serious student and received the best grades in his class. After graduation, he took a job as chemistry teacher in a small college.

Percy enjoyed teaching. But he hardly had time to work on his own experiments. His goal was to become a researcher. A researcher searches for more information about a certain subject and runs experiments to see how substances work together or under different conditions. He was disappointed that he could not get a full-time research job. In those days, around the 1920's, black chemists did not have the same opportunities for jobs that white chemists had.

Percy talked about his disappointment with his parents. His father said, "Don't let your skin color block your path to success."

Mrs. Julian told her son to keep his spirits up, that "Tomorrow will be more beautiful than today." His parents' advice gave Percy hope. He would keep on teaching. But he would not give up his dream of being a research chemist. A few years later, he studied at Harvard University and received an advanced degree. Then he returned to teaching.

Whenever Percy had free time, he read about new discoveries in science. Often, he worked late into the night. He knew that if he wanted to be a research chemist, he had to keep up with the latest experiments.

Julian knew that medicines often come from nature. Some medicines come from plants. Others can be developed from part of an animal's body. But animal parts were often expensive and hard to get. For

example, one medicine was made from the liver fluid of oxen. It took about 15,000 oxen to make a year's supply of medicine for only one person!

The chemistry teacher had an idea: What if he could imitate some of nature's cures? "If artificial medicines could be made cheaply, then everybody would have a chance for good health," he thought.

A famous chemist in Europe was doing research on creating artificial copies of natural substances. Percy wrote to the chemist, Ernst Späth. He told about his own experiments. Dr. Späth invited Percy to join him at the University of Vienna. Soon, Percy received the highest title awarded for university studies—a doctorate degree. Now he could be called Dr. Percy Julian.

Dr. Julian came back to the United States to teach and do research. He worked with other chemists to develop a medicine for the eye disease glaucoma (glaw KOH muh). Glaucoma can lead to blindness. It is caused by too much pressure building up in the fluids that circulate in the eye. The new medicine helped drain the extra fluid and prevent blindness. The success of Julian's research team was praised by doctors all over the world.

A large company in Chicago heard about Dr. Julian's experiments. The company was well known for its paint, food products, and chemical goods. Percy Julian was invited to be a director of research for the company. Many of their experiments were with soybeans. The soybean plant was a special interest of Julian's, too. The fruit of this plant is rich in vitamins and minerals.

One of the most exciting discoveries by Dr. Julian and his staff had to do with linking soybean research to a new medicine for arthritis (ahr THRY tihs). This disease affects the joints of people. Elbows and knees become stiff, swollen, and painful. Some people with arthritis become crippled for life.

A treatment for arthritis had already been discovered—a medicine called

cortisone (KAWR tuh zohn). Cortisone stops pain and reduces high fevers.

Cortisone is very expensive, however. Many people could not afford to buy it. Dr. Julian's team discovered a soybean-related substitute for cortisone. It was named "Compound S" and cost a lot less.

Thousands of people suffering from arthritis could now get relief for their pain. The lives of arthritis patients all over the world were improved.

The Julian research team found other uses for the soybean. They developed a substitute for an expensive dairy product used in making paint, glue, and plastics. The soybean product cost less than the dairy product. That saved the company thousands of dollars.

Foam for fire extinguishers is another product that comes from the soybean. The foam acts like a blanket, smothering fires. During World War II, the United States Armed Forces used the extinguishers to put out oil and gasoline fires. Many ships and thousands of lives were saved because of the foam.

From his earliest years, Percy Julian set high goals for himself—and reached them. But near the end of his life he told others, "I have had one goal in my life—to make life a little easier for the persons who come after me."

Percy Julian
(1899-1975)

Percy Julian received many awards for his research findings. His experiments were described in science journals all over the world. He eventually formed his own company that manufactured medicines. He continued to lead research efforts and later became head of another company that developed products from soybeans. Dr. Julian is often remembered for "opening the door" for other black scientists. His success gave many students the courage to pursue a career in science.

Music of Freedom

Pablo stepped back in shock. Security agents poured into his attic room. "You are against us, you—a *musician*!" growled one agent. "We will prove it and arrest you."

The soldiers began rifling through Pablo's papers. They searched his books. They went through his music. Pablo bit his lip in anger, but he did not say a word. What the agent said was true. He *was* against their government. Pablo believed that citizens should be able to live in

Pablo Casals lived for music and for freedom. Some governments didn't understand that.

freedom. These agents believed that only the government should have any say.

It was 1942 in Prades (prahd), France. Pablo had come to France from his native Spain three years earlier. Music had been his life in Spain. He played the cello and conducted an orchestra there. But when a ruler named Franco took over Spain, Pablo knew he could not stay. Franco's government did not care about freedom for the people. The musician fled to France and settled with friends.

From his room in Prades, Pablo wrote letters and planned cello concerts. Then the Nazis took over France. The Nazis and their leader, Adolf Hitler, wanted to take over the world. They did not care about people's rights. They did not allow disagreement.

Now there was no escape possible for Pablo, though. The Nazis would not let him travel. He could not give concerts—with the Nazis taking over France, Pablo refused to perform in public there. The Nazis were afraid he would help people fight them. They watched his every move. As the agents read his letters, Pablo stood quietly. He knew he could be arrested for no reason. He wondered if he would be shot.

Suddenly, the chief Nazi officer stopped searching. He turned to Pablo. "One day we will find what we are looking for," he said.

"And when we do, things will go hard for you." Without another word, he and the others left.

Pablo shook with anger as well as fear. He waited until the Nazis left. Then he sank to his knees. "Why treat an old man this way?" he wondered. "What secrets could I be hiding in my music? Do they think I have secret messages there about fighting their government?"

Pablo began gathering his papers and books. He would not dwell on his anger and fear. He had his music—music about peace and joy. At least he could *write* music and he could play music at home for himself and friends.

Life in Prades was hard. Pablo and the family he lived with were almost always hungry. They lived on boiled turnips and beans. When they were lucky, they found potatoes. Meat and milk went to the Nazis. So did coal and wood. Pablo wore his overcoat in the house, as well as outdoors.

The morning after the Nazis came, Pablo went out early. He was looking for sticks and branches to burn for fuel. He ran into his friend the poet, Ventura Gassol.

"Hello! Pablo!" Ventura yelled.

Pablo grinned. "Gassol, you shouldn't act like you know me. The Nazis will grab you out of these woods and shoot you."

"Nonsense," replied Gassol, with a wave of his hand. "We have too many friends. The Nazis wouldn't dare hurt us."

"I hope you're right," Pablo thought. He bent to pick up the sticks he had found. "Come to my house with me," he told his friend. "I have something to show you."

Pablo and Gassol climbed the narrow steps to Pablo's room. Pablo played his latest music piece. When he finished, Gassol had tears in his eyes. "It is beautiful, Pablo."

"Yes," Pablo sighed. He hoped some day a larger audience would hear it.

Suddenly Gassol laughed. "Pablo," he asked. "Do you remember the 'concert' we gave last year?"

Pablo laughed too. "Yes, indeed," he said.
"That was certainly music of a different
kind!"

He remembered when the two of them
had slipped out of their houses late that
night. Together, they walked to Mount
Canigou. They avoided well-lit streets and
hid in dark corners when soldiers came by.

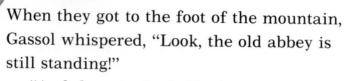

When they got to the foot of the mountain, Gassol whispered, "Look, the old abbey is still standing!"

"And there is the bell—the bell from the free people of Spain to the people of France," Pablo noted. "If we can ring it," he exclaimed with sudden hope, "people will know that the spirit of freedom is alive!"

"That's right, my friend," Gassol answered. "Let's start climbing."

"Of course, you know what will happen if the soldiers catch us," warned Pablo. Gassol nodded. Then he began to climb.

Gassol and Pablo climbed carefully to the top of the rickety old tower. Stones slipped out from under their feet. Pablo wondered whether they would fall. He hoped that no one had seen them leave town. Soon, he and Gassol reached the top.

"You are the musician. You must ring the bell," said Gassol. "I only hope it works."

Pablo gulped. It was just a bell, but the sound of it would be music to the people. He gripped the rope and pulled.

Out of the stillness suddenly rang music. The bell worked! Pablo laughed. "There it is!" he exclaimed. "The music of freedom!" He rang the bell again and again. For a moment, both he and Gassol forgot their danger. Then the sound of the bell died down.

"Let's get out of here," urged Gassol. He and Pablo scrambled down the tower and back to town.

The next morning, angry officials said that whoever had rung the bell was a criminal. They said anyone who was bad enough to ring the bell without official permission was bad enough to steal or even murder.

At this memory, Pablo just smiled. He knew that what had frightened those officials was only the sound of freedom. He had played that night for the people of Prades. And he had a feeling that they heard.

Pablo Casals
(1876–1973)

Pablo Casals was one of the greatest cellists who ever played. He conducted, wrote, and taught music as well. He often played music to raise money for the victims of war. He refused to play for unjust governments and people. Pablo Casals lived to be ninety-six years old and died in 1973. He spent his last years in Puerto Rico, and he kept up with his musical interests until he died.

Making a Promise

"A.D., where's your brother? Wasn't he out here in back with you?"

"Uh-huh, Daddy, he was." Seven-year-old A.D. King stopped tossing and catching his baseball for a moment. "But he went inside a while ago."

The Reverend King searched the large house for his middle child, eight-year-old M.L. The boy wasn't with his sister Christine or his mother or his grandmother. Finally his father found M.L. sitting on the front porch, reading a book.

"Excuse me, M.L., but I was wondering. You can't be the boy who's been begging for new shoes, can you?" he teased M.L.

Martin Luther King, Jr., had a dream that people would not be judged by the color of their skin.

123

M.L. looked up hopefully. "Yes, Daddy! I know just the kind I want."

"Yessir, this is the right boy. Well, how would you like to look in some stores? I finished writing my sermon for next Sunday. So I thought maybe I'd take a ride downtown. Do you want to go along?"

M.L. jumped up. "Just give me a minute to put away my book, Daddy. I'll be in the car before you get there." M.L. was careful with his books. He enjoyed reading as much as playing or talking. There were always new ideas and new words to discover.

M.L. had decided that he loved new words. As a preacher's son, he spent a great deal of time in church. He enjoyed listening to his father and other ministers preach. He saw how a good speaker could reach out to an audience. Someone with powerful words could charge people up and give them a renewed spirit. Someday, he hoped, he would be a fine speaker.

At the moment, however, all he was concerned about was a pair of new shoes. M.L. joined his father in the car and they drove toward downtown Atlanta, Georgia. It was 1937 and a shopping trip was an adventure. This was a time when not many people, white or black, had much money to spend. M.L. knew that his family was one of the better-off black families.

"Daddy," he asked, "why don't you and Mother go downtown more often? There are lots of stores here that I've never seen the inside of." He looked from side to side, delighted with the busy street. There were so many stores that he knew he would find what he was looking for.

"Well, M.L., let's just say it's easier to stay in our neighborhood."

M.L. could tell that his father was holding something back, but the boy didn't have time to ask that. "Look, Daddy, there's a big shoe store with lots of boys' shoes in the window. Can we go look?"

Reverend King found a parking space not far from the store. As they walked back to it, M.L. noticed a public drinking fountain and thought of taking a drink. But when he got closer, he saw a "Whites Only" sign on it. He walked past as if he had not seen the fountain at all.

At the shoe store, he looked carefully at the boys' shoes in the window. Soon he pointed out a pair. "This is it, Daddy. This is the style I want."

The Kings went into the store.

Then a man stopped them just inside the front door. Like all the salespeople in the downtown stores, he was white. "You'll have to go around and come in at the back of the store," he told them. "I can get to you in a few minutes."

Reverend King shook his head. "No, thank you, sir. This front part of the store is comfortable enough. We'll wait here."

At first the clerk thought the preacher didn't understand. "All colored use the back door," he explained. "You and your son can get served back there."

The Reverend shook his head again. "Either we'll buy the shoes here in the front of the store or we won't buy them at all."

Now the clerk was red with anger. "There are no exceptions to the rule. You take it like everybody else, and stop being so high and mighty!"

Playing to Win

One morning in the late summer of 1921, a thirteen-year-old boy stood in his front yard. His family had just moved to Beaumont, Texas, and he hadn't met anyone in the neighborhood yet.

Down the street he saw two barefoot girls racing toward him. One girl, about his age, ran on the sidewalk. The other, a bit younger, ran across the front lawns. Hedges grew between the houses and stretched to the walk. The girl hurdled each hedge and stayed even with the runner on the sidewalk. After hurdling the last hedge on the block, she put on a burst of speed and reached the corner several steps before the other girl.

Babe Didrikson Zaharias loved to compete. She became one of the greatest woman athletes in sports history.

"I whupped you again!" the hurdler cried. "I'm the fastest runner around."

"That's 'cause you get so much practice running away from Momma and Poppa," the other girl laughed. "You're always in trouble from one trick or another."

Then the girls noticed the boy.

"You're new, aren't you?" the hurdler said in a friendly tone. "My name's Babe, and this is my sister Lillie."

"Really her name is Mildred," Lillie added. "But all the kids call her Babe 'cause she hits home runs like Babe Ruth."

"My name's Raymond," the boy said.

"Can you play baseball, Raymond?" Babe asked. "If you do, you can come with us to the streetcar barn. Everyone gets together there for games."

"Thanks, but I don't think so," Raymond said. "I don't play with girls."

"Neither do we!" Babe hooted. "We play with the boys. Come on!"

In a vacant lot near the streetcar barn, a game had already begun.

"Hey, Babe," someone called. "You're on my team. Take over second base."

"Lillie, come over here. We're up," someone else yelled. "And the new kid can be on my team, too."

Few of the players wore gloves. Families in this neighborhood had little money for such luxuries. Babe ran onto the field. She caught a fly ball for one out, and then scooped up a grounder and shot it to first base for another out.

When it was Babe's turn to bat in the next inning, the pitcher couldn't strike her out. So, after four balls, Babe walked to first. From there she tried to "rattle" the pitcher.

"You better keep your eye on me," she yelled, " 'cause I can run faster than lightning. I can steal second while you're winding up. And then I'll just take third, too, for practice!"

Trying to ignore her, the pitcher threw the ball. The batter swung and knocked the ball into short right field. Babe was off

instantly. She rounded second and charged
toward third, where a boy twice her size
waited for the ball.

Her teammates saw the first baseman tag
the batter out and throw the ball to third.

"Slide, Babe, slide!" they yelled.

Without hesitation Babe slid, and her foot
touched the base just as the third baseman
stepped off the base to catch the ball. Safe!

There was blood on Babe's leg as she got
up. Raymond could see she was in pain. Her
team's leader noticed too.

"Hey, Babe, are you hurt? Do you want
someone to run for you?"

"You think I'd quit just 'cause of this little old scratch?" Babe demanded, clearly insulted. "I'm OK. Just see if I'm not! Let's play!"

A single brought her home a few minutes later. She limped in but said nothing. When her team took the field again, Babe ran out a bit slowly, but she played as hard and loudly as before. On her next at-bat, she hit a home run.

By the end of the game, Raymond realized he hadn't told anyone at home where he was going. He called good-by to his new friends and started running down

the street. Suddenly Babe was next to him.

"Race you to the corner," she challenged him.

He ran hard, but was two steps behind when Babe reached the corner and stopped for breath.

"You're pretty good," she told Raymond. "Usually Lillie's the only one who can stay close to me."

"Do you always have to race someone?" Raymond asked. "Does everything have to be a contest with you?"

Babe nodded. "Yep, I guess so. What's the fun of doing something if you can't find out if you're the best at it? And I aim to be the best athlete that ever lived."

Raymond laughed. "How can you manage that?"

"Well, to start with, I'm just naturally good at sports. And that's not just bragging—everyone'll tell you that. And second, I work hard. If I can't do something right off, I practice and practice and practice till I can do it, and do it the best!"

Raymond couldn't understand why he felt so friendly toward this girl. She was so full of herself! But she was also honest and funny and determined. And he liked talking to a girl who loved sports and didn't hide the fact. He knew that if he ever beat her in running or baseball or any other sport, it would be an honest win. She wasn't ever going to give in.

"Well, I can practice, too," he said. "And the next time we race, I'll beat you."

Babe smiled. "You can try. But you have to be pretty good to beat Babe."

Babe Didrikson Zaharias
(1911?-1956)

Maybe Babe Didrikson Zaharias did become "the best athlete that ever lived"—at least the best woman athlete. In 1932, she competed as a one-woman team in a national amateur track-and-field meet—and won! In the Olympics of that same year, she won two gold medals and a silver medal in track and field events. Babe excelled at many sports but became most famous in golf. She once won seventeen straight tournaments! She was active in establishing professional women's golf and won the United States Women's Open three times.

Sportswriters named Babe Outstanding Athlete of the Year six times. In 1950, they voted her the greatest woman athlete of the first half of the century. In 1953, it was discovered that Babe had cancer, an abnormal growth of cells in the body. She was operated on and came back to win five golf tournaments in 1954. She died of cancer two years later, in 1956.

Jackie Robinson was the first black baseball player in the major leagues. He became one of baseball's greats.

138

"We Need You Now!"

Jackie watched as the people walked to their seats in the great baseball stadium. The sound of music came across the field.

Another ballplayer stood next to Jackie. "You've got to win for us today, Jackie," he said.

Jackie looked at his teammate, Pee Wee Reese, in surprise. He wanted to ask Pee Wee what he meant. But just then the manager of their team, the Brooklyn Dodgers, began to talk.

"I don't have to tell you what this game means to us," the manager said to the team. "If we beat the Phillies today, we're sure of at least a tie for the championship. If we lose, the season could be over for us."

This was the last game of the 1951 season. The Dodgers were tied for first place with the New York Giants. If both the Giants and the Dodgers won their games today, or if they both lost, the season would end in a tie. But if only one of them won, the season would be over for the team that lost.

Jackie looked across the field and saw the umpire waving.

"Play ball!" the umpire shouted.

The game began. Jackie batted in the first inning, but did not get a hit. He came back to the dugout where his teammates were. "What did you mean when you said I had to win this game?" he asked Pee Wee.

"I mean you're our best player, Jackie. You've got to lead us."

Jackie listened to the crowd. The game was in Philadelphia, so the people were cheering for the Phillies.

The Phillies were soon leading the Dodgers by four runs. The score was six to two. Jackie was worried.

The scoreboard showed that the Giants were winning their game.

In the fifth inning, Jackie went to bat again. He picked up his favorite bat. His hands were sweating because he was nervous. He stood at the plate and looked

down to first base. One of his teammates
stood on first.

The Phillies' pitcher threw the ball.
Jackie swung and felt the bat hit the ball.
The ball sailed far into the outfield. Jackie
ran to third base with a triple. The player
who had been on first base scored easily.
Before the inning was over, the Dodgers had
scored three runs. Now the Phillies were
ahead by only one.

But when the Phillies came to bat, they
got two more runs. The score was now eight
to five in favor of the Phillies.

Just then a roar swept through the crowd.
Jackie glanced up at the scoreboard. The
Giants had won! Now the Dodgers had to

win or the season would be over for them. The Dodgers couldn't score in the next two innings. But in the eighth inning they scored three runs. The score was tied eight to eight! Now they had a chance to win the game.

The score was still tied at the end of nine innings. This would be an extra-inning ball game.

It was the twelfth inning! The Phillies had runners on first, second, and third with two out. If the Phillies scored a run, they would win the game.

Second baseman Jackie stood tensely between first and second base. He watched as the Dodger pitcher threw the ball.

The batter swung hard. The ball cracked against the bat and shot toward second base.

The fans in the stadium jumped to their feet.

Jackie ran desperately to his right. He knew he had to catch this ball or the Dodgers would lose the game. Just when the ball was about to go by him, he leaped into the air. His left hand, with the glove on it, was stretched out as far as it could stretch. While Jackie was still in the air, he felt the ball smack into his glove. He fell to the ground. The whole weight of his body crashed down on his right arm. His elbow smashed into his stomach.

He lay motionless on the ground, but the ball was still in his glove. The inning was over. The Phillies had not scored.

Jackie's teammates came running over and helped him off the field. His right arm, his stomach, and his right side hurt him terribly. He could hardly breathe.

The Dodgers could not score. When the Phillies came to bat again, the Dodgers ran out on the field—all except Jackie. Jackie lay on the bench, his face twisted with pain. Pee Wee came back into the dugout.

"Let's go, Jackie," Pee Wee said. "We need you now. We've never needed you more."

Jackie said, "I'm not sure I can help the team, Pee Wee."

"Remember what I told you?" Pee Wee said. "If you can't help, no one can."

Jackie struggled to his feet. Pee Wee helped him. Jackie put on his glove and went back on the field.

The Phillies could not score a run in the thirteenth inning. Then the Dodgers came to bat in the fourteenth inning. The first two players made outs. Now it was Jackie's turn to bat. The crowd fell silent as he stepped to the plate.

Jackie felt all alone. It was a feeling he knew well, for other reasons, too. Jackie had not made friends easily with the other Dodgers. Back in his early days, the others did not accept a black player as one of them. There were hard feelings and rude remarks, but things did get better. Now the team was counting on him. The pitcher raised his arms and threw. With his muscles tense, Jackie watched the ball. He swung with all his might as the ball crossed the plate. The bat met the ball with a crack.

Out, out the ball sailed—out toward left field and over the left field wall for a home run. Jackie ran around the bases and crossed home plate in triumph. The score was nine to eight! The Dodgers were ahead at last!

Jackie ran to the dugout. Pee Wee met him there. Both of them were laughing.

"You did it, Jackie!" Pee Wee shouted. "Now we'll win!"

Jackie Robinson
(1919-1972)

Jackie's home run won the game for the Dodgers. And even though the Dodgers lost their 1951 championship play-off to the New York Giants, Jackie Robinson's home run is remembered as a great moment in baseball history.

Jackie spent ten years with the Brooklyn Dodgers, starting in 1947. He helped them win National League championships in all but four of those years. Robinson's experience helped open the way for other black players in major league baseball. In 1962, Jackie Robinson was elected to the National Baseball Hall of Fame, an honor given only to the greatest baseball players.

Amelia Earhart loved adventure.
She flew flights no woman ever
had before.

No Place to Land

Amelia's tall, boyish figure cast a long shadow on the lawn as she hurried toward her house. Today, she was to start out to try what no woman had dared before. She was going to fly across the Atlantic Ocean alone.

Quickly, she gathered her flying suit, her maps, a toothbrush, a thermos of hot soup, and some canned tomato juice. This was all she allowed herself for the trip.

Just before leaving the house she looked out the window at the peaceful, familiar scene. On this beautiful spring day in 1932, the dogwood was blooming and her tulips were up. The grass was a beautiful soft green. In her heart she said a prayer that she might come back safely.

Soon afterward, Amelia was in the air, flying to Harbour Grace, Newfoundland, where she would begin her long flight across the Atlantic. A fellow pilot flew the plane while she saved her strength. They reached Harbour Grace the next day. Amelia rested at a hotel while her plane was prepared for the flight.

Early that evening, Amelia received word that her plane was ready. She dressed and went to the airfield. There she was handed a message. Amelia read it over and over again. Then she tucked the words from her husband, GP, into her jacket pocket and walked toward her airplane.

It was just after 7 P.M. when Amelia climbed into the plane. Soon the plane rose into the air. The wings glittered in the sunlight as the plane headed out to sea. She was on her way at last.

She wished GP could know how happy she was. He had said nothing, except that he had faith in her, but she knew that he was worried. She, herself, had no fear. No one could ask to have more of life than she was having.

She blinked her lights at a ship far below her, but the ship did not answer. She must be a mere speck in the sky, she thought, and no one had seen her.

Twilight faded. Amelia glanced at her altimeter. A moment ago it was showing how high she was. Now the hands of the instrument swung idly under the glass. The altimeter was broken! Now she would not be able to tell how high or low she was flying.

The night grew darker. Suddenly, Amelia heard the rumble of thunder above the roar of her engine. Almost at once a jagged streak of lightning split the sky.

A storm raged around the plane. Amelia pushed the plane's nose up, hoping to find calmer air.

She climbed steeply. But as the air grew calmer, the plane grew heavier. She looked at the windows. They were covered with frost. Ice formed on the wings. The plane

went into a sudden spin. It dropped lower
and lower—dangerously close to the sea.

Amelia gritted her teeth and pulled the
plane out of the drop, just in time. She could
see the waves breaking below her.

"Well, I got out of *that*," she said aloud.

Even so, the waves were much too close.
As soon as the ice melted on the wings,
Amelia lifted the plane again through the
mysteriously dark night. The storm still
raged, but she would have to fly through it.

The hours passed. Amelia studied the
instrument panel. She would not let her
mind rest on that broken altimeter.

Suddenly, out of the corner of her eye,
she saw a small tongue of flame outside,
coming from somewhere in the plane. This
was real trouble, Amelia knew. If only she
could land. But there was nothing but ocean
below her.

The flame flickered and died, and then
flared up again. She could only hope that it
would hold out until she could find a place
to land.

Hour after anxious hour she kept her
course, her eyes darting from the instrument
panel to the flickering flame. When dawn
came, the plane began to vibrate strangely.
She feared that at any moment something
might break.

By early morning, her neck felt stiff; her
legs were cramped. She was not hungry, but
she was thirsty. She punctured the can of
tomato juice and drank some through a
straw.

Amelia checked her reserve gasoline tank
and saw that gasoline was leaking to the
floor.

"Now I'll *have* to land soon," she said out
loud.

She scanned the stretch of water beneath her. There was not a bit of land anywhere, not a ship in sight. If her calculations were right, she would soon be near the middle of the Irish coastline. If! It was the biggest word in the world just now. She knew she could not last much longer. The altimeter was broken, the plane was shaking itself to pieces, the flame still burned, and now the gasoline was leaking!

At last, the dim coastline appeared out of the morning mist. Thank heaven! But where was an airfield? She circled, and flew up and down the coast, searching for one. There was no airfield . . . only tiny cottages, green meadows, and a few cows grazing on the lush grass.

She had to land somewhere!

Amelia circled again to find the best place to land. She hoped the cows wouldn't mind! The plane skimmed above the meadow. The cows grew larger and larger. Now they were as big as life just outside her window.

The plane came to rest gently on the broad field. Amelia sat quite still, her hands in her lap. She had done it!

Amelia Earhart
(1897-1937?)

Amelia Earhart made her flight across the Atlantic Ocean five years after Charles Lindbergh became the first man to fly across the Atlantic alone without stopping, in 1927. Then she became the first person to fly from Honolulu, Hawaii, to the United States mainland.

In 1937, the daring pilot tried to fly around the world. She almost made it. But when she was about halfway across the Pacific Ocean, heading for home, her plane vanished. Amelia Earhart was never heard from again.

With a Song in Her Heart

Fifteen-year-old Lucila looked in the mirror. She saw large green eyes and smooth bronze skin. Her high cheekbones were framed by two thick braids of hair.

Lucila wanted to make herself look older. She decided that the braids made her look like a schoolgirl. So she wound them up and pinned them to the back of her head.

"That's better. Now I look older, like a teacher should look!" Lucila said.

Even though Lucila was only fifteen, she had just been hired as a teacher's assistant. It was 1904. In the small villages of Chile, in South America, there was a need for teachers.

Gabriela Mistral was a teacher who wrote beautiful poetry.

"Do you think the children will respect me?" Lucila asked her sister, Emelina. "I am worried that they may not listen to me."

"You will be fine, Lucila. The children will love your songs and games. La Cantera is lucky to have you working in the school!" Emelina assured her.

Emelina was a teacher, too. Lucila's father had been a teacher and a traveling musician. He would roam the countryside, singing at festivals. From him, Lucila got her love of poetry and music.

When she was a baby, he made up rhymes and riddles. They often sang together. But her father was not happy.

He left the family when Lucila was three years old.

The school in La Cantera was twelve miles from Lucila's home. Every day she walked or rode horseback through a beautiful valley. She traveled along the winding Elqui River. The great Andes Mountains were in view.

Since she loved nature, Lucila did not mind the journey too much. She enjoyed the sights and sounds all around her. Wild flowers swayed in the breeze. Birds chirped happily above. Lucila sang out in her native language, "Todo el valle está danzado." ("All the valley is dancing.")

Lucila might begin in the morning by telling about the weather. Perhaps she would write out a poem or song for the children to copy. This way she would help them learn how to read.

For science, Lucila might take the class outdoors. She made everything in nature come alive. When the children looked at trees, she described them in a special way:

"The trees are fixed to the earth
with giant hooks beneath the soil.
They raise up their arms and
yearn for the sky."

Lucila's class had fun learning arithmetic. They gathered leaves, stones, and acorns. The children had to count everything and write their numbers.

For history, Lucila might read stories about famous people. She let the class act out events.

After lunch the children ran outdoors. Lucila called out, "En un corro bajo el sol!" ("Together under the sun!") She asked the children to pretend. They danced like wheat swaying in the field. Or they raced in circles like swirling rivers.

At the end of the day, Lucila reminded them, "Learning and loving nature are the most important things in life, children."

When she returned home in the evening, Lucila might spend hours writing. She wrote down happy songs and rhymes. She also wrote some sad poems. She thought about people who had died or moved away. She missed her father, and knew she might never see him again.

The years passed and Mama and Emelina were very proud of her. In due course, Lucila passed a test to become an official teacher. She moved around to different schools, bringing her energy and enthusiasm with her. Lucila wanted her students to love learning, and she always expected them to work hard. At night, she continued to write her poetry.

"Your poems are so beautiful, little sister," Emelina reminded her. "In Santiago, there are newspapers and magazines. Maybe you can send your poems to them."

"I want to share my poems with other people," Lucila thought. "But I am afraid that some school officials will not like their teacher writing such poems."

Lucila thought a moment and then her face lit up. "But I can use a pen name. Then nobody will know it's me!" She ran over to the mirror. "I must look at myself carefully. I will think of another name. I want a name that will show the spirit in my heart."

Lucila stared at her face in the mirror. Then she smiled. "I will call myself 'Gabriela' after the angel Gabriel, a messenger of good news. And my last name shall be a word that describes the wind—'Mistral.'

"Gabriela Mistral—that is a beautiful name!"

One day Lucila learned about a major poetry contest for all the poets in the country.

"Lucila, you have a chance to win the gold crown for poetry!" a friend exclaimed. "The judges will be well-known authors and officials. Everyone will know your work if you win!"

Lucila took a deep breath and dared to enter the contest. It seemed like forever, but finally the special day arrived. Prizes for the poetry contest were being awarded. The judges met in a large hall to announce the winners. Lucila sat quietly in the balcony. She was very nervous.

When the time came to hear about the first-place winner, the hall became very quiet. Lucila closed her eyes. A judge stood up and began speaking. "We will now read the poems of the first-place winner. The name of the poet is Gabriela Mistral!"

Her heart was pounding so hard, Lucila thought it would burst. Tears came to her eyes. To herself, she cried out, "I won! My heart is singing, I am so happy. Now Gabriela Mistral's words will live on forever."

Gabriela Mistral
(1889-1957)

Gabriela Mistral went on to win many prizes for her poetry. Huge crowds turned out to hear her speak. Her poems were translated into many languages and published all over the world. In 1945, she became the first Latin-American writer to win the world's highest honor for literature, the Nobel Prize. Nobel Prizes are awarded each year for achievements in science, literature, and peacemaking. Prizewinners are people who have helped the world become a better place through their work.

Gabriela Mistral's work as a teacher became known all over South America. The government of Chile gave her special jobs. In 1922, the government of Mexico asked her to help improve Mexico's education system.

Jim Thorpe's Indian name meant "Bright Path." He could play every sport, and play it well.

"The Greatest Athlete in the World"

You could feel the excitement in the air on that beautiful July day. It was 1912 in Sweden, the time of the Summer Olympics! Thirty thousand people came to watch and cheer, even the king and queen. They looked on from the royal box as the track-and-field events began.

For months, sports fans everywhere had been waiting for the Olympics to begin. Everyone wondered how that fabulous Indian, Jim Thorpe, would do.

Then "that Indian's" name was announced: "And from the United States, Jim Thorpe." The Americans in the audience rose to their feet and roared.

Jim, who was part Sauk and Fox Indian,
spent his childhood in Oklahoma. His
Indian name, Wa-tho-huck, meant "Bright
Path." Young Jim Thorpe could play
anything. And he could play better than
anyone else. He was especially good at
track-and-field sports.

When the coaches at the Carlisle Indian
School in Pennsylvania discovered Jim's
athletic ability, they put him on the track,
football, and basketball teams.

Before Jim left for school, his father
said to him, "Son, you are an Indian. I want
you to show people what an Indian can do."

"I will, Father. Just wait and see," Jim
responded.

And now here Jim was in the Olympics.
The things he was doing were way beyond

his father's wildest dreams. If only his father were still alive to see him.

Jim was about to begin the pentathlon (pehn TATH lahn), a track-and-field event with five parts. The first part was the broad jump. Jim went over the jump in his head. He pictured himself at the mark, then running, then taking off like an eagle.

When Jim's turn came about, the Americans burst into cheers. Then the crowd grew silent. When Jim was ready, he took off running. The audience was shocked by his incredible speed and the grace of his body as he soared to his winning jump. The Americans jumped to their feet in celebration. Their Jim Thorpe had won the first part of the pentathlon!

Jim went on to win first place in the 200-meter dash, the 1,500-meter race, and the discus throw. He came in third in the javelin throw. Winning four out of the five parts, he won the gold medal for the pentathlon.

Six days later, Jim began competing in the decathlon (dih KATH lahn), a ten-part track-and-field event. The decathlon lasted three long days. The competitors were tiring by the third day, except Jim. He got stronger with each part of the event. When it was over, Jim had placed first in four of the parts. Again he had won the gold!

"He's a horse! He's a horse!" echoed throughout the stadium.

On the last day of the Olympics, King Gustav presented the awards to the gold medalists. When the king announced Jim's name, the crowds cheered wildly.

While shaking his hand, the king said to Jim, "Sir, you are the greatest athlete in the world."

A wonderful feeling rushed over Jim. He was embarrassed and nervous, though. All he could say was "Thanks, King," in a mumbling voice.

Back in the United States, crowds greeted Jim. Parades struck up the band. Reporters tagged along everywhere. Everyone wanted to see the young Indian athlete.

"How did it feel when the king said, 'You are the greatest athlete in the world?' " one reporter asked.

"It was the proudest moment of my life," Jim answered.

Next it was back to school for one more year, and then—who could say? This Olympic star's future surely would be a "bright path."

Then it happened. No one knows exactly how the story came to light. Jim's world suddenly came crashing down, though. First there were the rumors. Newspapers followed up on them. They uncovered a story that Jim had accepted money in the past for playing baseball. Olympic athletes were supposed to be amateurs—that is, they were not to take money for playing.

A few years before the 1912 Olympics, Jim had a summer job playing baseball. He was paid a small salary, and he played for pay the next summer as well.

Being a professional in one sport—that is, taking money for playing—made him a professional, the Amateur Athletic Union said. The union wanted Jim to return his gold medals.

Jim couldn't believe it.

"Why should a summer baseball job stop me from being an Olympic track-and-field champ?" he wondered bitterly. "Besides I never made a secret of the baseball job."

The young athlete remembered something that his father had told him about a famous leader of the Sauk and Fox.

"Son, you are a lot like the great Black Hawk. You have his dark eyes and skin. Your hair is the same black color. You have his strong will and his talent.

"Black Hawk was the greatest leader of our people. He won many battles. But when he lost, he lost with honor. You must follow his example. When you lose, you, too, must lose with honor."

Jim tried to remember these words every time he lost a game. He knew he deserved the gold medals. Hadn't he proven himself to be the best athlete in the world? Surely the union was making a mistake. But what choice did he have? "Give the medals back, Jim," his trainer, Pop Warner, advised. "Rules are rules, and athletes need to play by rules."

Jim understood that his honor was at stake here. And so, he would lose this round with honor. In his own eyes, and those of his fans, though, he still was the "world's greatest athlete."

Jim Thorpe
(1888-1953)

Jim Thorpe became a successful professional baseball player *and* a professional football player. He played for many different teams. He donated time and money whenever he could to help Indian causes, too.

For years, people tried to get the union to change its decision. But no one was successful until Charlotte Thorpe, Jim's daughter, made up her mind to get Jim's honor back as an Olympic athlete.

Nearly thirty years after Jim died, the Olympic Committee decided that he had won his gold medals as an amateur in 1912 after all. In 1982, the committee voted to put Jim Thorpe's name back in the Olympic record books and to give copies of his medals to his family.

F·i·n·g·e·r S·i·g·n·s

Helen Keller was locked in a dark, silent world. Her teacher helped her to escape.

When Helen woke in the morning, she could tell that something special was supposed to happen. She didn't know what it was, but she felt the excitement around her. Mother took extra care to dress Helen nicely. After breakfast, Helen ran outside her Alabama home to wait. Although she didn't know why, she began to get excited too.

It was 1887 and Helen was almost seven years old. But Helen couldn't do most of the things that other seven-year-old children could. She had been blind and deaf for five years. She lived in complete darkness and

silence. She made signs with her hands and arms when she wanted or needed something. She would push for "go" and pull for "come," or she would pretend to cut bread if she was hungry. But she was often misunderstood.

Helen knew she was different from other people. She realized that others didn't use her signs when they wanted something. When she stood between two people she could feel their lips move. Helen thought this very strange. Because she couldn't hear, she didn't know that they were speaking, and because she couldn't see, she didn't understand that they were talking. Sometimes Helen would try to move her lips, but she grew angry when nothing happened. She would scream and kick until she fell asleep.

As Helen grew, so did her desire to communicate with others. The few signs she made were not enough anymore. She became angrier at her world each day. Helen was growing up lonely and wild because no one knew how to teach her.

Some people believed that Helen was just not smart and that her parents ought to put her into an institution for sick people. Her tantrums scared them. They thought she was dangerous. But Helen's parents knew better. They knew that her tantrums were

the result of a smart child locked in a dark,
silent world. Yet, they didn't know how to
help her.

Captain and Mrs. Keller tried many times
to find help for their daughter, but the
answer was always the same. "Helen will
always be blind and deaf. There's nothing
we can do." Then one day the Kellers heard
about a special school that could send a
teacher to Helen. This was the cause of the
excitement. Today was the day Helen's
teacher would arrive.

When the carriage arrived, Captain
Keller rushed out. He helped the young
teacher, Miss Anne Sullivan, down. She
introduced herself and immediately began
searching for her new pupil. Miss Sullivan
saw Helen waiting on the porch. Her face
looked angry, and her eyes stared into space.

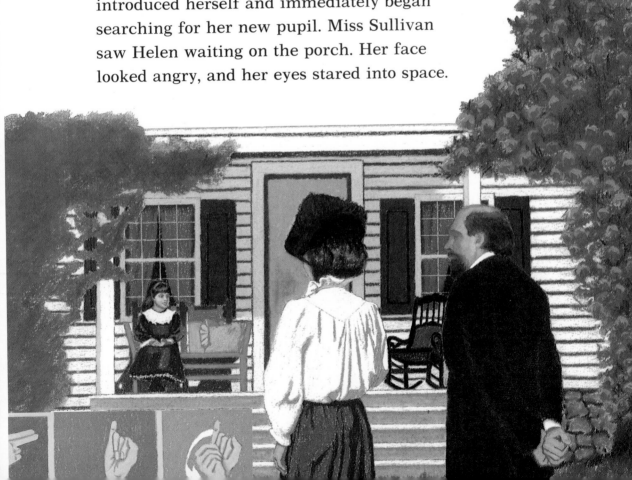

Helen could feel the vibrations of footsteps approaching her. She put out her hand, expecting her mother to take it. The hand that took hers, however, was unknown to Helen.

The next day, Miss Sullivan gave Helen a doll. While Helen was playing with the doll, Miss Sullivan made strange finger signs into Helen's palm. Miss Sullivan was teaching Helen how to spell the word *d-o-l-l* in the finger alphabet of the deaf. Helen was curious about what this stranger was doing, so she sat very still. After Miss Sullivan made the signs a few more times, Helen was able to repeat them back to her. She had no idea that she had just learned to spell her first word. Helen did not yet understand what a word was, or that words were the way people spoke with one another.

Helen also did not know that Miss Sullivan had come to teach her. She only knew that a stranger had entered her house and took control of her life. At first, Helen was angry. Her family had always let her do what she wanted for fear of hurting her. But this stranger wasn't giving Helen her own way. She didn't understand why Miss Sullivan was there, so Helen fought her.

Helen's family found it hard to understand, too. They wondered if Miss Sullivan was expecting too much from Helen. She was, after all, blind and deaf. Miss Sullivan relieved their doubts. "Helen must know we love her, but we cannot let her think she is different because she is blind and deaf. She must behave herself."

Miss Sullivan and Helen did many things together in the following weeks. They took walks through the garden and forest. Helen learned how to knit and string beads. For everything Helen did, felt, or smelled, Miss Sullivan made a finger sign in Helen's hand. Helen learned to spell quite a few short words in this way. But still she did not understand that these finger signs were words.

She did not know that the finger sign for
m-u-g meant the thing that she drank from.

One day, Miss Sullivan and Helen strolled
through the garden and stopped at the water
pump. Miss Sullivan put Helen's hand under
the running water from the pump and
formed the signs for water into Helen's
other hand. She repeated the word *w-a-t-e-r*
over and over. Helen stood as still as a
statue. She felt the finger signs being
repeated on her hand, and slowly became
aware that those signs meant the cool
something that was running over her other
hand. She understood her first word!

Helen was so excited. She ran everywhere touching things—the ground, the porch, Mother, Father, Teacher, and demanded to know the words. She learned how to spell them all. Helen wasn't just repeating meaningless signs anymore. She was learning words. She was understanding language. Helen felt her world come alive.

Helen Keller
(1880-1968)

Helen Keller became blind and deaf because of an illness she had when she was about one-and-a-half years old. Although Helen started learning much later than most people do, it did not take her long to catch up. When she was almost ten she began learning how to speak, even though she hadn't heard speech since she became ill.

Determined to go to college, Helen entered Radcliffe College in the fall of 1900. Miss Sullivan attended classes and spelled the lectures into Helen's hand. A teacher gave Helen her exams, but no other special arrangements were made for her. She graduated with honors at a time when not many women at all graduated from college.

Helen devoted her life to teaching people about the blind. She urged the government to have more books printed in braille. (See the story about Louis Braille on pages 218-225.) She raised money to help the blind. And she wrote books and spoke widely about the special needs of blind and deaf people.

Emily Gowan Murphy helped win rights for women in Canada.

Dear Canada

"Whoa, Ginger, stop here!" The driver jumped from the carriage. He helped the five passengers down. Turning to the tall gentleman, he said, "Well, Parson, this will be your home in London for a time." It was 1898, and the Murphy family had just arrived in England for the parson's new job assignment.

Parson Murphy thanked the driver. He
smiled at his wife, Emily. "My dear, this
surely is far from our family and friends in
Canada. But let us make the best of our time
here in London. Two years shall go by
quickly."

The parson then spoke to the children.
"Evelyn, Kathleen, Doris—all must pitch in

already beginning to fall out. Soon the disease will spread to my whole jaw."

Anger welled up in Emily's body. She asked more questions. "Why are the factories so dangerous? Who owns them? Why can't city officers stop such things?"

In her diary, Emily wrote about the unlucky woman. She also wrote about her to family and friends in Canada. She told them about other problems she saw in London.

"Raggedy children live outdoors. Soldiers, who were wounded in the war, are homeless and begging. Who will help these people?"

Emily's heart was filled with pity. She could not turn away and forget the problems. "All people should have the

chance to live a good life. They should not have to wear rags or beg for food."

She was also angered by the difference between the rich and the poor. Finely dressed citizens rode in shiny carriages. At the same time, people slept under bridges and searched for food in garbage barrels.

Time flew by for the Murphy family. Emily's diary was getting thicker. She wanted to share her experiences with more than just family and friends. She decided to write a book so that all of Canada would know about what she was seeing.

One evening, Emily told her idea to her husband.

"My dear," said Parson Murphy, "your idea is a fine one. However, I am worried what the people who pay my wages will think. A parson's wife can be caring, but not so outspoken."

Emily spoke with a strong voice, "It's not fair that women cannot speak out. If men can become mayors and judges, why not women? Someday our world will change. I will find other women in Canada to take part in those changes!

"I know you mean well, Arthur," she continued. "I certainly do not wish to ruin your job. So I will write my book, but use a pen name. Let us think of another name to use for the author."

" 'Johnny Canuck' is used to describe somebody born in Canada. Why not use that name?" Parson Murphy suggested.

His wife replied, "I like 'Canuck.' But I want to write as a woman. 'Janey Canuck' will please me just fine."

So Emily began to write her book. She used her diary for ideas, and she was sure that people in Canada would want to read about what she had seen.

Later, when Emily's book was published, she was overjoyed. "My book will be a success," she declared happily.

The family's stay in London was almost over. The family looked forward to arriving home and seeing familiar places. But a few years after settling back home, the Murphys set out once again for new scenes. This time they would stay in their own country and move to Manitoba, in Canada's West.

In the early 1900's, the western part of Canada was much like the early West in the United States.

The girls clapped and jumped with glee. "We will ride horses! We will hike out in the country!"

Emily sighed. "Children, farming is hard work. And we shall be busy helping others. Maybe I'll keep a diary," she added thoughtfully. "People in Canada's West will have problems, too. Janey Canuck can come along. She will help me speak out."

Emily Gowan Murphy
(1868-1933)

Emily Gowan Murphy served as Canada's first woman judge from 1916 to 1931. Before that, she was known for her magazine and newspaper articles. She wrote on many subjects and urged women to speak up for themselves. She also worked to change Canada's laws so women could have more rights. Emily's writings told about life as she saw it. She described the good and the bad. *The Impressions of Janey Canuck Abroad* and *Janey Canuck in the West* became well-known books.

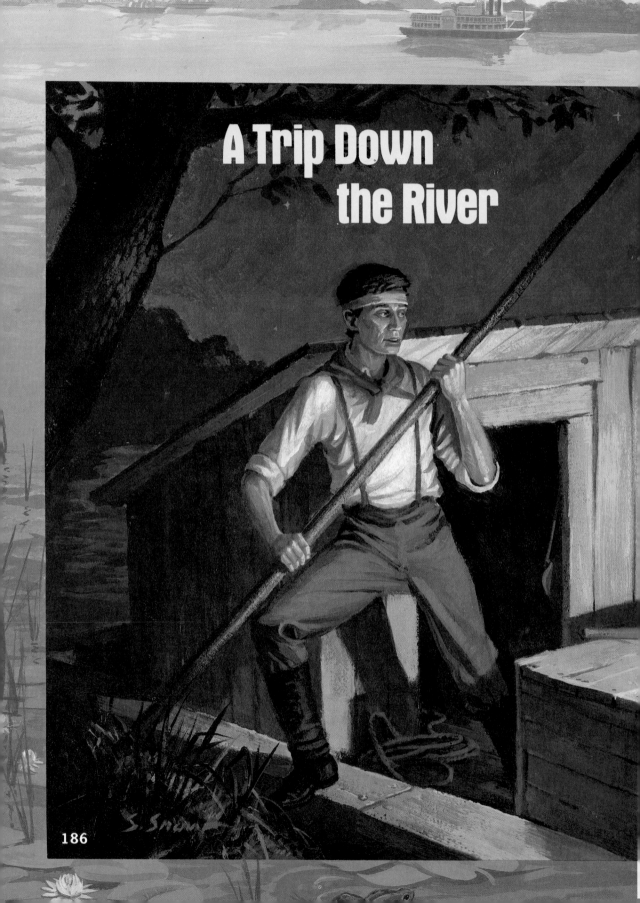

A Trip Down the River

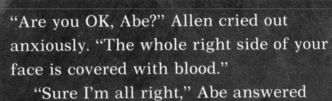

"Are you OK, Abe?" Allen cried out anxiously. "The whole right side of your face is covered with blood."

"Sure I'm all right," Abe answered calmly. He wrapped a piece of cloth around the deep cut over his right eye. It was the kind of cut that would leave a scar for life.

"I guess my father knew what he was doing when he hired you to come with me on this trip down the Mississippi," said

Abraham Lincoln took a trip to New Orleans when he was a young man. He saw things he would not forget.

Allen. "Back in Indiana, everyone knows that Abe Lincoln can't be beaten in any kind of fight or wrestling match."

The two young men started putting their boat back in order. Moments ago robbers had crept onto their boat and tried to steal the farm goods they were planning to sell in New Orleans. Abe and Allen were sleeping, but surprised the thieves by acting quickly and tossing them off the boat!

"We'd better get out of here in case the robbers decide to come back," Abe said firmly.

"But Abe," Allen protested, "you know it's dangerous to try to float down the Mississippi River in the dark."

"We'll have to take our chances out on the water. It's not safe enough to stay here any longer," Abe insisted.

And so, the two young men pushed off silently from the shore aboard the flatboat Abe had helped make with his own hands. They had come so far—about 1,200 miles

(1,900 kilometers)—from their home in
Spencer County, Indiana. Allen's father,
James Gentry, had hired Abe to help Allen
float his farm goods down to New Orleans.

They were getting close to the city now.
In New Orleans, Allen and Abe would have
a chance to see the grandest city along the
Mississippi River.

It was 1828, and nineteen-year-old Abe
Lincoln had never ventured so far from
home. And what a journey it was! Not only
were they almost robbed at one point, but
there were storms and sand bars and tricky
currents, too. And the greatest adventure
still lay ahead in New Orleans.

One steamy day on the wide, lazy river
flowed into another. Abe and Allen pushed
quietly along and waited hopefully. Finally,
before their very eyes, the great bustling
port city came slowly into view. Hundreds of
other flatboats and steamboats clogged the
harbor. Huge ocean-sailing ships towered on
the horizon. Abe wondered how close they

were to the sea and how far the great ships had come.

Both young men were awed and nervous in all the noise and confusion. Nevertheless, they found a place to tie up their boat and busily set about organizing their goods for sale. There would be so much to do and see!

The next day, Abe and Allen sold Mr. Gentry's produce plus the goods they had traded for along the river. Then they broke up their boat and sold the lumber. With some of the money they made, they bought tickets for a steamboat ride back home to Indiana.

But it was not time to go home yet. They spent a few days wandering around. They roamed the narrow streets of the crowded city, seeing more people in an hour than they might see in a year back home. New Orleans was filled with sailors from all parts of the world. French, English, Spanish, Italian, Greek, Portuguese, and Chinese—the city was alive with different languages and cultures.

In a part of the city called the French Quarter, Abe and Allen looked with wonder at the fancy iron grillwork outside the beautiful houses. But the one sight that truly sent shivers up their spines was the famous slave trading that they saw in the New Orleans markets.

"I know that you were born in a slave
state, Abe. But did you ever see anything
like this?" Allen asked.

"I was only seven when we moved from
Kentucky to Indiana. I remember seeing
slaves in fields and I've seen slaves traded
before—but nothing like this," Abe replied.

Gangs of slaves were herded through the
streets in chains. Slaves were bought and
sold like farm animals and forced to work
for their owners. They had no rights of their
own, no freedom. Many of the slaves worked
on huge farms called plantations, raising
cotton. Abe and Allen had seen stacks upon

stacks of the fluffy raw cotton all over the harbor area. It was brought to market here in New Orleans.

"Look over there," Abe whispered to Allen at one of the slave auctions. "It looks like a mother is being sold to one owner and her children are being sold to different owners. And that man with his hands tied has deep cuts on his back. Maybe he was whipped for trying to escape."

"Until today, I never thought much about slavery," Allen said. "I've just figured it was a way of life in some places."

Abe agreed. He wondered about what it really would be like to own people as if they were cattle and force them to work without pay.

The two young men made their way thoughtfully to the boat at the end of their

stay. Abe's head was filled with the scenes of slaves he had just viewed. Years later, he would write about seeing other slaves chained together on a riverboat: "That sight was a continual torment to me. . . . (slavery as such) has the power of making me miserable."

Lincoln had no way of knowing that the problem of slavery would start to tear the nation apart in the future. But he had seen the horror of slavery up close in 1828, and it had given him plenty to think about. Now it was time to go home.

Abraham Lincoln
(1809–1865)

Abraham Lincoln earned twenty-four dollars making this trip for Mr. Gentry in 1828. Not long afterward, he moved with his family to Illinois and began to study law. Lincoln became a powerful political leader in later years, when the country became very split over whether to allow slavery to spread. He was elected President in 1860. As President, Lincoln issued the Emancipation Proclamation in 1863, which led to the freeing of the slaves.

Clara Barton always wanted to help people. She worked as a nurse and founded the American Red Cross.

"I Can't Walk."

"Oh, please let me do something for him," Clara begged with tears in her eyes. "How can I help?"

"You're only a child," her mother said, leading Clara back into the kitchen. "You can help most by doing your lessons and staying out of the way." Clara's older brother David had been injured in a serious fall. He was in too much pain to walk now.

Clara found it hard to keep her mind on spelling and geography, especially when the doctor came. There was a murmur of voices from David's room. Clara strained her ears, trying to hear what they were saying. But they spoke too softly.

When the doctor came out of David's room, he spoke in low whispers to Clara's mother. Then he gathered up his things and went off to visit his next patient.

"Will David be all right, mother?" Clara asked as soon as the doctor had gone.

"We don't know yet, Clara," her mother answered. "The doctor said that David must be kept very quiet and that he must have lots of care."

"Can't I help David get well?" Clara asked. "There must be something I can do to help."

Clara's mother did not answer right away. She knew that with all her other chores she would have little time to give David the special care he needed. But was Clara old enough and strong enough to be her brother's nurse? She was only about eleven years old.

"Very well, Clara," her mother said at last. "You may try to help."

During the weeks that followed, Clara spent every free minute in David's room. She arranged his pillows and gently sponged

his face with cool water. She fed him the
beef broth her mother made. She read to
him. And sometimes she just sat quietly next
to his bed.

Clara's father was worried because Clara
never played outdoors anymore. She was
getting pale.

"You must not spend so many hours with
David," he told her one day. "Sometimes you
must have fun and do the things you enjoy
doing so much."

"But taking care of David is what I like
to do best," Clara answered.

"You can still take care of David, but I
want you to go riding on your horse once in
a while," her father said.

After that she often took short horseback rides. But she always hurried back to David as soon as she had finished riding. Clara's father watched the color slowly coming back to her cheeks, and he was satisfied.

At last, the day came when the doctor said David could get up from his bed. The patient stood up, and took one shaky step. Beads of sweat glistened on his forehead. David tried to take another step, but instead he sank down to his knees.

"I can't," he gasped. Tears stung his eyes. "I can't walk!"

"You'll be able to walk soon," Clara said. She pretended not to see her brother's tears as she helped him back to bed. "Your legs have just forgotten how, that's all."

More than ever Clara spent her time at David's bedside. She was his nurse and he was her patient. She was determined that David would walk again.

Weeks went by. Clara never tired of staying with her brother.

She talked to him. She read to him. She tried to assure him that he would walk soon. But months passed and David still wasn't well. Clara did a good job of raising her brother's spirits. She knew he still was weak though, and in too much pain to walk.

The Barton family was desperate. Would David ever walk again?

Then one day Clara heard her father
talking to someone whose voice she didn't
know. She peeked out into the hall. "A new
doctor," she guessed, seeing the man's black

case. Mr. Barton spotted Clara and introduced the stranger to her.

"My daughter, Clara, Dr. McCullum," Mr. Barton said. "Dr. McCullum has come to try to help David, Clara. I've been telling him how devoted you've been to your brother." The doctor smiled at Clara warmly.

Later that day, the doctor asked the Bartons to let him bring David to his home for special treatments. He thought that perhaps David had lost too much blood while sick and had simply become too weak. During those days it was common medical practice to draw blood out of sick people, using leeches. The doctor also thought David might need a different diet.

"But David might not have lasted this long without you, Clara," he said to her. He said that she did a wonderful job of keeping her brother's spirits up.

Good news came in time. David's pain lessened under Dr. McCullum's care. He was able to try walking again. Clara was there one day when her brother swung his legs over the side of the bed.

"Just lean on me," she offered.

David put one hand on Clara's shoulder, but he seemed afraid to move. Clara slipped her arm across her brother's back and braced herself.

"Now!" she cried. "You can do it! I know you can!"

David swayed to his feet, gritted his teeth, and took a step. He staggered. But Clara's arm was firm across his back. Slowly he took another step—and then another.

Step by step, David walked across the room. Clara smiled up at her brother. At last he was really well.

Clara Barton
(1821-1912)

Clara Barton grew up to become a famous nurse. This story took place in Massachusetts sometime between 1833 and 1835.

Years later, the American Civil War broke out between the Northern and Southern states. Clara went to the battlefront to deliver hospital supplies and to help nurse the sick and wounded. She saved hundreds of lives and gave comfort to those in need. The soldiers called her "The Angel of the Battlefield." After the war, she continued to help people suffering from wars or disasters. Clara Barton became famous as the woman who founded the American Red Cross, an organization of volunteers who help people in time of disaster.

Even as a girl, Harriet Tubman knew she had to fight slavery somehow.

Young Hattie

One fall evening around 1835, a woman stood at the door of a slave cabin on a plantation in Maryland. Rit and her husband and several of their children lived in this one-room shack with no windows. Rit was watching a figure run smoothly down the path toward her. She called inside to her husband. "Ben, Harriet's coming."

Harriet was about fourteen years old. Her master had hired her out to a neighbor to work in the fields. She was barefoot and wore a faded, shapeless dress.

"Hey, Mama," she greeted Rit. "Master and Missus Barrett sent me to the Big House with a message. They don't know how fast I can run, so I got some time for a visit."

"Want a bite of hoecake, Hattie?" her mother offered.

though. It fell far short and landed on Harriet's head. With a moan, the girl fell to the floor, unconscious.

The overseer stepped over her body and ran out to look for the runaway. The other slaves clustered around Harriet.

"Did you see how she stood up to him?" a man asked wonderingly. "Hattie got herself killed to free someone else."

"She ain't dead yet!" a woman cried, trying to stop the flow of blood.

"Oh, Lord," someone prayed, "leave this child with us. We need her courage."

"Amen," another joined in. "If young Hattie acts like this now, think what she'll do when she's a woman!"

Harriet Tubman
(1820?-1913)

Harriet kept up her fight against slavery. Years after this story took place, she ran away to the North, where there was no slavery. Harriet returned to Maryland time after time, though, and helped other slaves escape. During these years there was a whole group of people helping and hiding escaping slaves on their way to freedom. The helpers called themselves the Underground Railroad. Young Hattie became the railroad's most famous "conductor."

Father Miguel Hidalgo y Costilla led his people in a fight for freedom. He is now known as the Father of Mexican Independence.

The Grito de Dolores

"Padre, there are officials coming up the road! I think they are here to arrest you. What shall I do?"

Father Hidalgo (ee DAHL goh) looked up to see a farmer from the village. The man was trembling with fear. He had seen Spanish authorities beat—and even kill—people. He was afraid for Father Hidalgo.

The priest rose with a smile. "Don't worry, my son. No one can take away what we have begun. Our projects will go on."

Father Hidalgo was the priest of a church in the small town of Dolores (doh LAWR uhs) in northern Mexico. Soon after arriving there in 1803, he decided he wanted to do something to help the poor people of his parish, especially the poorer Indians. Spain had conquered Mexico in 1519-1521. When this happened, Mexico became "New Spain," part of Spain's American empire. The Spanish leaders had not been treating the natives of New Spain well. They were particularly harsh to the Indians, forcing them to work long, hard hours.

Father Hidalgo began several projects to help the Indians improve their condition. He bought a small piece of land near his church and hired Indians to plant crops. They planted mulberry trees, the leaves of which are used in making silk. And they planted grapevines for wine. Hidalgo set up a blacksmith shop, a carpenter shop, a silk industry, and a place for making pottery.

The priest knew that the king of Spain had forbidden the colonists of New Spain to make certain goods like silk and wine. These goods were made in Spain for trade with New Spain. The king feared that if the colonists started making such goods, they would stop trading for the ones made in Spain. But Hidalgo was sure he could bring

his people a better life. And he was right. The people of Dolores had gained pride as they worked.

Father Hidalgo wondered why the officials had been sent. Then the priest's thoughts were interrupted by a harsh voice.

"Are you Father Miguel Hidalgo y Costilla (ee kohs TEE yah)?" an officer asked.

Father Hidalgo was startled. "Yes, I am Father Hidalgo," he answered.

The soldier's face reddened. "Father," he said gruffly, "I am ordered to destroy your illegal crops."

And without another word, the authorities began killing the crops. First, they attacked the mulberry trees. They pulled up saplings by the roots. Twigs snapped under the horses' hoofs as they stomped through the groves.

Then they slashed the tender young grapevines. They tore the grapes off the vines and tossed them to the ground. Soon there was nothing left.

The priest remained silent until the officials had left. Then he went to the church. He rang the bell to call his people together. Then he spoke.

"My friends," he said, "by now perhaps you know that our trees and vines have been destroyed. But I beg of you, do not lose hope. We will go on. We will rebuild."

For more than two years, Father Hidalgo worked on his projects. He kept the workshops going, but nothing seemed to help.

"No matter how hard we work," he told his friend Ignacio Allende, "Spain takes everything away from us."

"I am afraid that nothing will change," Allende replied. "Not until we are free of Spain."

Then, suddenly, New Spain got its chance. In 1808, the French pressured the king of Spain into giving up his throne, and a time of unrest and confusion began in Spain. Some people in New Spain decided that this would be a good time for New Spain to try to overthrow Spanish rule. New Spain could make a surprise break for freedom and the Spanish leaders wouldn't be prepared. Before long, Father Hidalgo and his friends started making plans.

In the fall of 1810, however, they found themselves in danger. Doña Josefa María de Domínguez, another supporter of independence, learned that officials of the Spanish government planned to arrest Father Hidalgo and his group. Doña Josefa sent word.

The priest was not afraid. "My friends," he said, "the time has come. We cannot wait for freedom and we will not flee. I shall call my people together!"

The brave priest walked swiftly to his beloved church. He climbed the steps to the bell tower and began ringing the heavy church bell.

When the people of Dolores heard the bell, they came out into the streets.

Soon the people gathered at the large stone church. There Father Hidalgo spoke to them of the government's harsh treatment and of the need to be free. "My children," he said, "the time has come. Will you be free?" Then he cried out, "Down with bad government! Long live freedom!"

The priest's "cry of Dolores"—the *Grito de Dolores*—spread through the crowd. The people shouted back with joy. Soon, thought Father Hidalgo, his message would spread throughout all of Mexico.

The priest knew that the war for freedom would be hard. But he was sure that his people would win. The Mexican revolution against Spanish rule had begun. And Father Hidalgo had helped make it happen.

Father Miguel Hidalgo y Costilla
(1753-1811)

Father Hidalgo did not live to see his people finally win freedom in 1821. In 1810 and at the start of 1811, he led his soldiers against Spanish troops, but they could not stand up against the well-trained Spanish army. Early in 1811, the priest was captured by the Spanish and put to death in July of that year. Nevertheless, the Mexican people honor Miguel Hidalgo y Costilla as "The Father of Mexican Independence." Each year, they reenact the *Grito de Dolores* and remember the priest who helped them seek freedom.

Louis Braille was a blind person with a dream: to read and write. He made his dream come true for all blind people.

Magic Dots

Laughter echoed down the halls of the large, stone-walled school building. Boys were greeting one another happily. Like other students throughout the city of Paris in the early 1820's, these boys were returning from their long summer vacation.

Amidst the laughter and excitement, a young boy walked alone. Although deep in thought, he heard the sound of footsteps and the tapping of a wooden cane approaching him. The tapping was a familiar sound in the school. These boys were blind. They used canes to find their way. The school, located in Paris, was the Royal Institution for Blind Youth.

The boy felt a hand on his shoulder. Then he immediately knew the clear, warm voice of his good friend Gabriel.

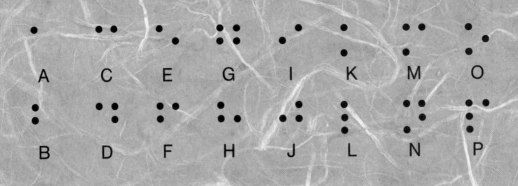

A C E G I K M O

B D F H J L N P

alphabet. He also made patterns for the numbers one to ten.

"This will work!" he exclaimed.

Louis couldn't wait to show the other boys. The moment he arrived back in Paris, he called for Gabriel. Louis wanted him to be the first to try his discovery.

Gabriel was excited. "We can write each other notes and letters," he shouted.

Quickly, the news of Louis' new alphabet spread through the school. Everyone rushed to Louis' room to try the "magic dots."

"Look!" exclaimed one boy. "Already I can write my name. This is so simple."

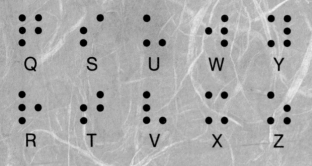

Q S U W Y
R T V X Z

What would your name look like if you spelled it in braille? By using 1 to 6 dots in different patterns, Louis Braille was able to make a code for the alphabet, numbers, and short words.

Another boy told Louis, "I could never do my arithmetic because I kept forgetting those long lists of numbers. Now, I can write the numbers on paper."

Louis was thrilled by his classmates' reactions. He couldn't help reminding them, "Now we can read! My dream has come true. There will be books for the blind!"

Louis Braille
(1809-1852)

Louis Braille became blind because of an accident in his father's shop when he was three years old. He invented his basic touch system of reading and writing when he was fifteen years old, in 1824.

Louis grew up to become a teacher at the Royal Institution for Blind Youth. He also became famous in Paris as a musician. He played and composed music for the organ.

Louis' greatest disappointment was that so few people had a chance to learn his "braille" system. Two years after he died in 1852, the school finally adopted Louis' system. Today blind people throughout the world read and write braille.

Maria Mitchell loved to study the skies. She discovered a comet, and shared her love of science with others.

Miss Mitchell's Comet

In some ways, fall in New England in the 1840's was like fall in New England still is today. The leaves changed color. Children went back to school. Young men went back to college. Young women, however, did not go to college.

In those days, many people believed that too much education would hurt a girl's health. They believed that if a young woman could read and write, she had all the education she could take.

Maria Mitchell's parents encouraged her to learn, however, and Maria was glad they did. Maria was twenty-nine and the oldest of the Mitchell children living at home.

"I almost wish we weren't having a party tonight," Mr. Mitchell told his wife one fall morning in 1847. "The weather will be clear.

I will envy Maria standing on the roof, looking at the stars."

Mr. Mitchell chuckled. "How I remember when Maria was just a little girl, and I let her work with me. She was so quick to learn how to handle the telescope! When she was old enough for college, I should have told her to dress up like a boy and enroll. She would have enjoyed the classes so!"

"William!" Mrs. Mitchell gasped. "What an idea! Maria should be thinking of marrying. Play-acting as a boy, indeed!"

Maria laughed as she entered the room. "Don't worry, Father," she said. "At the library, I get to read all the latest books and articles about astronomy and mathematics."

She cleared the table and straightened up the room. The rest of the morning Maria spent studying. In the afternoon she hurried off to her job as a librarian. She liked helping other people find out what they wanted to learn. Besides, the job gave her a chance to read books and to hear lectures on many topics.

But Maria liked astronomy even more. As early as she could remember, her father had a telescope. He set it up on the roof of the family's home on Nantucket Island, off the coast of Massachusetts. By the time she was twelve, she was his trusted assistant. Now

Maria and her father used a larger telescope.
They worked as partners "sweeping" the sky.

When sweeping the sky, astronomers
examine one part of the sky after another
in a regular pattern. They compare what
they see in the sky to charts made by earlier
observers. They make additions to the charts.
They watch for changes and keep careful
records of what they see.

That evening, October 1, began as usual.
Maria chose a section of the sky above the
North Star. She had looked at it many times
before and knew what to expect. Tonight,

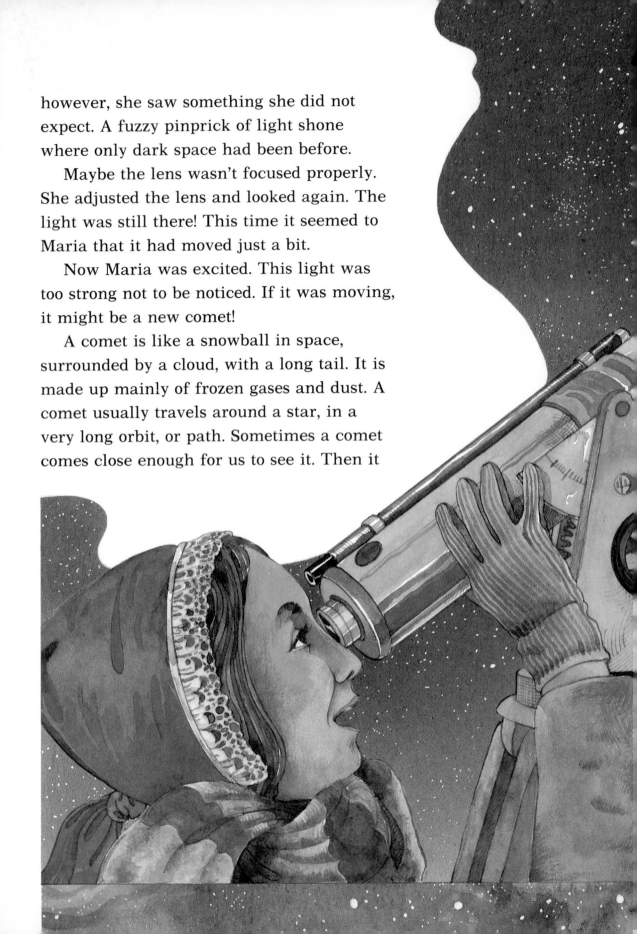

however, she saw something she did not
expect. A fuzzy pinprick of light shone
where only dark space had been before.

Maybe the lens wasn't focused properly.
She adjusted the lens and looked again. The
light was still there! This time it seemed to
Maria that it had moved just a bit.

Now Maria was excited. This light was
too strong not to be noticed. If it was moving,
it might be a new comet!

A comet is like a snowball in space,
surrounded by a cloud, with a long tail. It is
made up mainly of frozen gases and dust. A
comet usually travels around a star, in a
very long orbit, or path. Sometimes a comet
comes close enough for us to see it. Then it

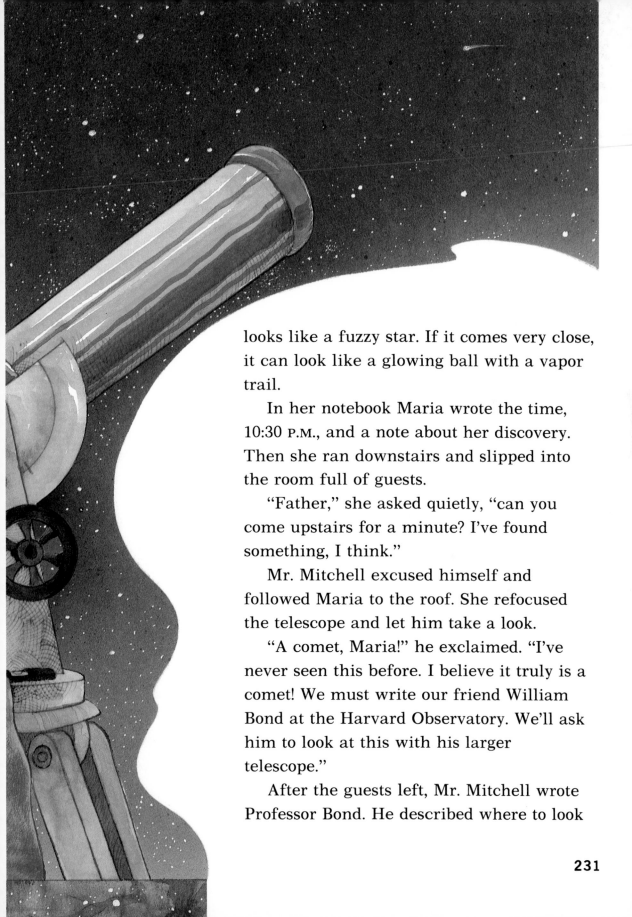

looks like a fuzzy star. If it comes very close, it can look like a glowing ball with a vapor trail.

In her notebook Maria wrote the time, 10:30 P.M., and a note about her discovery. Then she ran downstairs and slipped into the room full of guests.

"Father," she asked quietly, "can you come upstairs for a minute? I've found something, I think."

Mr. Mitchell excused himself and followed Maria to the roof. She refocused the telescope and let him take a look.

"A comet, Maria!" he exclaimed. "I've never seen this before. I believe it truly is a comet! We must write our friend William Bond at the Harvard Observatory. We'll ask him to look at this with his larger telescope."

After the guests left, Mr. Mitchell wrote Professor Bond. He described where to look

for Maria's comet. Then Maria and he
waited. Had she really discovered a comet?

Soon Professor Bond wrote back. Yes, he
had found Maria's spot of light. And, yes,
it *was* a new comet! Professor Bond said
also that he had sent the news of Maria's
discovery to an astronomer who worked for
the king of Denmark.

Several years earlier, the king of
Denmark had announced a prize. A gold
medal would go to the first person to see
and report each new comet. Professor Bond's
report of Maria's discovery went to the
judges who would award the medal. Other
astronomers reported sighting the comet,
too. But, after reviewing their information,
the judges announced that Maria had been

the *first* to see the new comet. Therefore, the comet would be named after her—Comet Mitchell. This was the first time that a comet was named for a woman.

One evening, Maria showed her medal to her visiting nieces and nephews.

"What do those words on the medal say, Aunt Maria?" one of her nephews asked.

"The words are in Latin," she answered. "They say 'Not in vain do we watch the setting and rising of the stars.' Here at the bottom is the date, October 1, 1847, and my name is printed around the edge. The medal is beautiful, isn't it? Now would you like to see something even more beautiful?"

And Maria led her nieces and nephews up to the telescope on the roof and let them take turns looking at the stars.

Maria Mitchell
(1818-1889)

Maria Mitchell was the first woman member of the American Academy of Arts and Sciences and of the American Association for the Advancement of Science. Both organizations still study scientific questions today.

In 1865, when Vassar College opened as one of the first women's colleges, the self-taught Mitchell became a professor of astronomy there. During her twenty-three years as a teacher, she inspired hundreds of young women to take up careers in science.

A Mission of Courage

It was 1753. Robert Dinwiddie was the acting governor of Virginia, a British colony. "The French are moving onto land that belongs to Great Britain," Governor Dinwiddie told twenty-one-year-old George Washington as they sat in the governor's office in Williamsburg, Virginia. "You are to go and warn the commander of the French forces that they must leave. The French must stay clear of the western country. Deliver this letter to him."

Young George Washington took a message to a French commander during colonial times. The mission almost killed him.

"Easy to say," Gist grunted. "We're not well fixed for building a raft, with only one small hatchet between us."

For one long day, George and Gist took turns chopping down small trees and hacking away their branches. They bound the logs together with vines they stripped from trees. Then they pushed the raft into the raging Allegheny. They leaped aboard, each carrying a long pole to guide the clumsy craft.

Jagged chunks of ice crashed against the raft. Then ice began to pile up behind it, threatening to destroy it.

"I can stop this!" George shouted to Gist as he jammed his long pole deep into the muck of the river bottom. Then he pulled on the pole with all his might. That would halt the raft, he thought, and allow the ice to slide past. Instead, disaster struck.

The river's current was too swift. It
pushed the raft so hard against the pole that
it lashed forward, pulling George with it. He
was thrown into the frigid, muddy water.

Gist froze with fear. He fought to keep
his balance on the violently bobbing raft as
he strained to see George.

There he was. With a superhuman effort
George kept his head above water. One large
hand grabbed a log of the raft and hung on.
Then he struggled to pull himself back onto
the raft.

The raft was still caught in the ice-filled
river, and the two men were not able to get
it to either shore. Near a small island they
left the raft and waded ashore.

George had been saved from drowning.
Now he was in danger of freezing to death.
George and Gist pounded off the ice that
covered them from head to toe. They spent

the night on the island, moving about, to keep from freezing.

"If we'd gone to sleep last night," said Gist the next morning, "both of us might well be dead now."

Looking out over the river, they learned that the freezing weather had actually done them well. Now the Allegheny was completely covered with ice, solid enough to hold their weight. They crossed the ice and continued south.

On January 16, George reached Williamsburg. The next day he gave the governor a written report on his journey. He wrote about the growing French threat.

"I hope my conduct on this mission has been satisfactory to you," George said at the end of his report.

Governor Dinwiddie assured the young soldier that he had done much more than just well. George was promoted from major to lieutenant colonel in the Virginia army.

In the spring of 1754, George led a group of soldiers sent to protect a new fort that the British built. But French soldiers captured the fort before George's forces could reach it. The threat of war loomed in the North American wilderness.

Then the French captured another British fort, Fort Necessity. Fighting at Fort Necessity began a war between British and American armies against the French. It is called the French and Indian War. The British and Americans won the war and a peace treaty was signed with France in 1763. For a while, at least, the British could say that much of North America was theirs.

George Washington
(1732-1799)

George Washington took part in some of the fighting in the French and Indian War. Later, Americans declared independence from Great Britain, and Washington became commander in chief of the American armies. He led them to victory in the Revolutionary War. In 1789, Washington became the first President of the new nation, the United States.

Sequoyah was a Cherokee Indian.
He invented a system of writing
for his people.

242

Sequoyah's Secret Marks

A group of Indian boys crowded around a man who sat alone by a small fire.

"There he sits—the dreamer! Sequoyah (sih KWOY uh), who makes magic with marks," the boys yelled.

At Sequoyah's side were some strips of bark from a tree. Now and again he drew a mark on the smooth side of a piece of bark with a sharp stick.

"I do not make magic," Sequoyah said. "I am making a 'talking leaf' such as the white man has. He makes marks on what he calls paper. These marks are his thoughts."

The boys shook with laughter.

Sequoyah became angry. As he stood up, he tucked something into his wide belt.

"Yes, Sequoyah will take the words of the Cherokee people and turn them into marks on a piece of bark," the leader of the boys,

"Sequoyah" is sometimes spelled "Sequoya."

243

Young Hawk, said. "Then others will look at the marks and understand what they say. He calls these marks talking leaves."

Young Hawk held some bark to his ear.

"This talking leaf says nothing. It is as foolish as Sequoyah."

He tossed the bark into the fire. Then the boys kicked the other strips into the fire. Sequoyah tried to stop them, but the bark was now a heap of ashes. Sequoyah's years of patient work had been for nothing.

Young Hawk cried out, "The chiefs here in our village talk about Sequoyah and what

he does. They say he is a magician, and for that he may be punished."

Just then, a drum beat loudly. It was the call to a council meeting. Everyone had to go to the meeting.

Sequoyah worried. What was the council about? Did Young Hawk speak the truth? Were the chiefs about to punish him? Would his dream of putting Cherokee thoughts down on bark be ended?

By the time Sequoyah arrived at the council ring, the rest of the villagers were already there. They whispered as Sequoyah came near the circle.

Now the drum beat for attention, and Sequoyah's name was called.

The chief, Bear Man, spoke. "Sequoyah, we hear bad things about you. We hear that you make magic. And that you will bring evil to the Cherokee people. Are these things true, Sequoyah?"

"No, they are not," Sequoyah answered.

"And the marks you make, Sequoyah? Do they speak to you?" Bear Man asked.

Sequoyah nodded his head. "Yes, but not out loud. You cannot hear them—you must see them. I will show you."

Sequoyah pulled a knife from his belt and began to trace some of the strange figures in the hard, packed earth.

Bear Man looked at them closely. "These silly marks tell me nothing," he said. "You are a fool."

"Please," Sequoyah begged. "You will understand if I show you more. Ahyokeh (eye OH kay), my daughter, has watched me. Let me show her some marks. If she knows what it says, you will know I tell the truth."

Bear Man sat in silence.

Trembling, Sequoyah spoke again. "I will tell you—in your ear alone—what a word will be. If Ahyokeh does not tell you that word, then you may punish me."

Bear Man did not answer. The waiting was almost unbearable. Sequoyah's heart pounded.

Then Bear Man spoke. "Send for Ahyokeh."

When Ahyokeh came, Sequoyah drew some more strange marks on the ground.

"Ahyokeh, look well upon these marks," Bear Man said. "What do they say?"

Shy and frightened, Ahyokeh hung her head. Sequoyah strained to help her.

"Ahyokeh, look, remember! I told you what this was. Think, Ahyokeh."

"I don't know," Ahyokeh said. "I can't remember. Father said it was a word, a Cherokee word."

Bear Man pointed for Ahyokeh to leave the council ring. The council was over. Sequoyah would be punished.

Just then, Ahyokeh's face brightened. She ran back to Bear Man. "The word was 'Cherokee,'" she cried.

"Sequoyah has spoken truly. This is the word he told me," Bear Man said. "Now he will tell us about the talking leaves."

"The secret is here," Sequoyah said. He drew something from his belt. It was the thing he had tucked away when the boys came upon him. It was a small piece of bark with a few rows of marks carefully written on it.

"The talking leaf says nothing if you do not know the marks. But it is not magic. The

Cherokee people speak with sounds. These marks are signs for each sound we use. Together they make words. It is the way the marks are placed that so many words can be said.

"The white man has marks like these that all the people know. I want the Cherokee to have talking leaves of their own." Sequoyah looked around at the chiefs in the council ring. "For many years I have listened to Cherokee words to hear the sounds. I heard all the sounds and made a mark for each one. Now when I say a new word, I can write it in these marks. I will teach the marks to the Cherokee. Then we will have talking leaves of our own."

Sequoyah waited a little and continued. "But today, all my words were burned. I must write them all again, and I must make sure each sound has a different mark. It will take a long time."

Bear Man stood up and said, "This is not a crazy man or a magician. Sequoyah will teach us. Some day Sequoyah will give great things to the Cherokee people. I, Bear Man, believe this to be so."

The council was ended.

Sequoyah
(1760?-1843)

Bear Man's words came true. Sequoyah gave his people a system of writing that used the Cherokee language. There are different versions of Sequoyah's story and how he introduced his way of writing. But we do know his work was destroyed at least once and that he had trouble getting the other Cherokee to listen to him. This story is set in Georgia. Sequoyah completed his system in 1821, after several years of work.

Sequoyah made it possible for the Cherokee to open their own schools and to print their own newspapers. Some Cherokee still use Sequoyah's writing today.

Books to Read

There are many good books about notable people and the subjects for which they are famous. A few are listed here. Your school or public library will have some of these, as well as many others.

■ Ages 6–8

George Washington by Ingri and Edgar Parin d'Aulaire (Doubleday, 1936)

A simple, classic picture book about the life of America's first President.

The Many Lives of Benjamin Franklin by Aliki (Prentice-Hall, 1977)

This delightfully illustrated picture book tells of Benjamin Franklin's varied life as a writer, printer, politician, and diplomat.

Martin Luther King Day by Linda Lowery (Carolrhoda Books, 1987)

A well-written account of the first official celebrations of this great leader's birthday. His life and the events leading to his death are also discussed.

Mother Teresa, Friend of the Friendless by Carol Greene (Childrens Press, 1983)

An easy-to-read biography of the Nobel Peace Prize winner who has helped thousands of poor people throughout the world.

The Sky Is Full of Stars by Franklyn Branley (Crowell, 1981)

A fascinating introduction to astronomy. Included is information on some of the brightest stars and constellations: how to find them and how they came to be.

A Weed Is a Flower: The Life of George Washington Carver by Aliki (Simon and Schuster, 1988)

A beautifully illustrated read-aloud biography of the slave-born scientist who developed all kinds of new products through plant research.

■ Ages 9–12

Babe Zaharias by Elizabeth Lynn (Chelsea House Publishers, 1988)

A touching biography that captures the true personality of this great woman athlete.

The Cosmos by Mat Irvine (Silver Burdett, 1986)

A brief yet thorough description of our solar system, galaxy, and the cosmos. A wonderful book filled with colorful photographs, diagrams, and paintings.

Dorothea Lange: Life Through the Camera by Milton Meltzer (Penguin, 1986)

A nicely written biography of Dorothea Lange, an American photographer whose photographs of poor families in the 1930's helped create support programs for them.

Flight: A Panorama of Aviation by Melvin Zisfein (Knopf, 1981)

A beautifully illustrated and comprehensive history of flight.

How to Think like a Scientist by Stephen Kramer (Crowell, 1987)

A very interesting book that helps you ask the right questions and sort out facts when you're trying to figure out how things in nature work.

Lincoln: A Photobiography by Russell Freedman (Houghton/Clarion, 1987)

The words and photographs work together to make this book an important reference on Lincoln as well as enjoyable reading.

Louis Braille by Stephen Keeler (Bookwright Press, 1986)

A well-written biography of this inventor, musician, and teacher who invented the Braille system for the blind.

Mark Twain: What Kind of Name Is That? by Robert Quackenbush (Prentice-Hall, 1984)

An enjoyable introduction to the life of one of the most famous American authors.

My Life with the Chimpanzees by Jane Goodall (Pocket Books, 1988)

What is it really like to live among the chimpanzees in Africa? This wonderfully descriptive book will tell you.

Round Buildings, Square Buildings, and Buildings That Wiggle like a Fish by Philip M. Isaacson (Knopf, 1988)

Striking photographs make this book a lively introduction to the world of architecture.

Stars by Seymour Simon (Morrow, 1988)

An astronomy book containing beautiful photographs and illustrations and including information on black holes, pulsars, and quasars.

The Story of Jackie Robinson, Bravest Man in Baseball by Margaret Davidson (Dell/Yearling, 1988)

A revealing look at the life of one of baseball's great players.

To Space and Back by Sally Ride and Susan Okie (Lothrop, 1986)

This beautifully photographed book takes readers on a journey into space on the space shuttle. Enjoyable for readers of all ages.

Up From Slavery by Booker T. Washington (Airmont, 1967)

A moving autobiography that describes Washington's rise from slavery to national distinction as a leader and an educator.

New Words

Here are some words you have met in this book. Many of them may be new to you. All are useful words to know. Next to each word, you'll see how to say the word: **architect** (ARH kuh tehkt). The part in capital letters is said more loudly than the rest of the word. One or two sentences tell what the word means.

architect (ARH kuh tehkt) An architect is a person who designs buildings of all types. He or she may draw the plans, select the materials, and oversee the builders.

astronaut (AS truh nawt) An astronaut is a crew member of a spacecraft.

astronomer (uh STRAHN uh muhr) An astronomer is someone who studies the planets, stars, and other heavenly bodies.

author (AW thuhr) An author is a person who writes books, stories, plays, poems, or other works.

black hole (blak hohl) A black hole is an unusual place that may exist in space. It is an area where gravity is so strong that anything pulled into it cannot get out again.

boycott (BOY kaht) To boycott means to refuse to buy or to use the products or the services of a country, business, or person so as to show displeasure.

braille (brayl) Braille is a system of reading and writing used by blind people. Raised dots are arranged in patterns. A different pattern is used for each letter of the alphabet.

chemistry (KEHM uh stree) Chemistry is the science that deals with the substances that make up the universe. It examines the way elements act, change, and combine with each other and with other things.

comet (KAHM iht) A comet is a frozen ball of ice, gas, and dust that travels around a star in a very long path. It looks like a star, but has a long tail of light.

decathlon (dih KATH lahn) A decathlon is an athletic contest made up of ten different track and field events.

dehydrated (dee HY dray tid) Dehydrated means that all the water or moisture has been removed from something.

engineer (ehn juh NIHR) An engineer is a person who is specially trained to design and build structures, machines, and other products.

gravity (GRAV uh tee) Gravity is a natural force that draws things toward the earth's surface or toward each other.

missionary (MIHSH uh nehr ee) A missionary is a person who is sent by a religious group to teach religion or to help set up schools and hospitals.

mission specialist (MIHSH uhn SPEHSH uh lihst) A mission specialist is a highly trained scientist who comes along on space flights to complete a specific task.

musician (myoo SIHSH uhn) A musician is someone who is good at singing, playing a musical instrument, or writing musical composition.

Nobel Prize (NOH behl pryz) The Nobel Prizes are awards given each year for outstanding achievements in science, literature, and peacemaking.

nun (nuhn) A nun is a woman who enters a religious order and devotes her life to prayer and helping others.

Olympics (oh LIHM pihks) The Olympics are contests in summer and winter sports that are held every four years for athletes from around the world.

orbit (AWR biht) To orbit means to circle the earth or another planet or heavenly body along a steady path.

pentathlon (pehn TATH lahn) A pentathlon is an athletic contest made up of five track and field events.

physicist (FIHZ uh sihst) A physicist is a person who studies physics, the science that deals with how everything in nature works. Physicists study heat, sound, gravity, energy, and all kinds of questions about how the universe is made.

plantation (plan TAY shuhn) A plantation is a large farm in a warm area. Usually, only one kind of crop is grown.

prime minister (prym MIHN uh stuhr) A prime minister is the head of the government in certain countries.

remote manipulator arm (rih MOHT muh NIHP yuh lay tuhr ahrm) A remote manipulator arm is a giant robot arm used on space flights that is controlled from the spacecraft by an astronaut. It allows the astronaut to grab objects, such as satellites, from space and bring them to the spacecraft.

rocket booster (RAHK iht BOOS tuhr) A rocket booster is a rocket engine that helps push spacecraft away from the earth.

satellite (SAT uh lyt) A satellite is a machine that "works" in space. It may take pictures and measurements that help us understand space and forecast weather. Others send television and telephone signals worldwide.

space shuttle (spays SHUH tuhl) A space shuttle is a spacecraft that looks something like an airplane and can be used over and over.

Supreme Court justice (suh PREEM kawrt JUHS tihs) A Supreme Court justice is a member of the highest court in the United States.

universe (YOO nuh vurs) The universe is everything that exists, including the earth, the planets, the stars, and outer space.

Illustration Acknowledgments

The publishers of *Childcraft* gratefully acknowledge the courtesy of the following photographers, agencies, and organizations for illustrations in this volume. When all the illustrations for a sequence of pages are from a single source, the inclusive page numbers are given. Credits should be read from left to right, top to bottom, on their respective pages. All illustrations are the exclusive property of the publishers of *Childcraft* unless names are marked with an asterisk (*).

Cover: Aristocrat and Standard Bindings—Victor Valla (top), Wende Caporale (middle), Lyle Miller (bottom)
Heritage Binding—Toby Gowing; Ron Vesely*; Penelope Breese Gamma/Liaison*; Floyd Cooper; Wende Caporale; Carolyn Ewing; Scott Snow; Wende Caporale; Victor Valla
Discovery Binding—Roberta Polfus

2–3: Lydia Halverson
10–11: Scott Snow
12–13: Stephen Shames, Visions*
14–15: Scott Snow
16–17: Stephen Shames, Visions*; David Gamble, *Time Magazine*
18–19: Wende Caporale
20–21: NASA*
22–23: NASA*; Wende Caporale
24–25: NASA*
26–31: Victor Valla
32–33: Ron Vesely*
34–39: Carolyn Ewing
40–41: Carolyn Ewing; Joe Traver, Gamma/Liaison*
42–43: Lyle Miller
44–49: Canapress*
50–55: Allen Davis
56–57: Penelope Breese, Gamma/Liaison*
58–61: Karen Loccisano
62–63: Karen Loccisano
64–65: Margaret Miller*
66–67: Floyd Cooper
68–69: © Ezra Stroller*; © J. Barry O'Rourke, The Stock Market*; © Nathaniel Lieberman*
70–71: © Dennis Brack, Black Star*; I.M. Pei and Partners*
72–73: National Center for Atmospheric Research/National Science Foundation*; C.C. Pei from I.M. Pei and Partners*
74–75: Yoshi Miyake
76–77: Yoshi Miyake; Mary Ellen Mark Library*
78–79: Yoshi Miyake
80–81: Yoshi Miyake; UPI/Bettmann Newsphotos*
82–87: Lydia Halverson
88–89: UPI/Bettmann Newsphotos*
90–95: Victor Valla
96–97: Victor Valla; TCMA Ltd. 1982–4*
98–103: Marie DeJohn
104–105: Marie DeJohn; AP/Wide World*
106–111: Steven Schindler
112–113: Steven Schindler; UPI/Bettmann Newsphotos*
114–119: Arvis Stewart
120–121: Arvis Stewart; AP/Wide World*
122–127: Floyd Cooper
128–129: Floyd Cooper; AP/Wide World*

130–135: Carolyn Ewing
136–137: Carolyn Ewing; UPI/Bettmann Newsphotos*
138–143: Michael Hays
144–145: UPI/Bettmann Newsphotos*
146–151: Yoshi Miyake
152–153: Yoshi Miyake; UPI/Bettmann Newsphotos*
154–159: Toby Gowing
160–161: Toby Gowing; AP/Wide World*
162–167: Isidre Mones
168–169: Isidre Mones; UPI/Bettmann Newsphotos*
170–175: Wende Caporale
176–177: Wende Caporale; American Foundation for the Blind*
178–183: Allen Davis
184–185: Allen Davis; Pollard Collection, P4127/A3355, Provincial Archives of Alberta*
186–191: Scott Snow
192–193: Scott Snow; Library of Congress*
194–199: Karen Loccisano
200–201: Karen Loccisano; American Red Cross*
202–207: Steven Schindler
208–209: Steven Schindler; Library of Congress*
210–215: Michael Hays
216–217: Michael Hays; © Robert Frerck*
218–223: Lydia Halverson
224–225: Lydia Halverson; Culver*
226–231: Arvis Stewart
232–233: Arvis Stewart; Maria Mitchell Observatory*
234–239: Marie DeJohn
240–241: Marie DeJohn; Jointly owned by the National Portrait Gallery, Smithsonian Institution and the Museum of Fine Arts, Boston*
242–247: Yoshi Miyake
248–249: Yoshi Miyake; Granger Collection*

Index

This index is an alphabetical list of the important topics covered in this book. It will help you find information given in both words *and* pictures. To help you understand what an entry means, there is sometimes a helping word in parentheses. For example, *Challenger* (space shuttle). If there is information in both words and pictures, you will see the words *with pictures* after the page number. If there is *only* a picture, you will see the word *picture* before the page number.